(*The Living Organization*)

SPIRITUALITY
IN THE WORKPLACE

William A. Guillory, Ph.D.

Published by Innovations International, Inc., Publishing Division
310 East 4500 South, Suite 420
Salt Lake City, Utah 84107 USA
(801) 268-3313 TEL
(801) 268-3422 FAX
Email: Innointl@cris.com

A Spiritual Experience

*"It is highly significant, though gener-
ally a neglected fact, that those creations
of the human mind which have borne
preeminently the stamp of originality and
greatness have not come from within the
region of (personal) consciousness.*

*They have come from beyond con-
sciousness, knocking at its door for admit-
tance; they have flowed into it, sometimes
slowly as if by seepage, but often with a
burst of overwhelming power."*

G. N. M. Tyrrell

I was abruptly awakened on the morning of October 3, 1985, at 1:30 A.M. I had an overwhelming urge to write "something." So I got out of bed, went over to my hotel room desk, and began writing without conscious thinking. Words flowed *through* me at a rate with which I could hardly keep pace. There were phrases and concepts I had never heard of before, pouring into my consciousness. Then, just as abruptly as this process started, it stopped. So I went back to bed as if in a trance. The next morning when I awakened, I read phrases that challenged my most fundamental beliefs about reality, such as: "mankind's descriptions of life are all illusions;" "there is no meaning, only being;" "time is an illusion as are all other forms of man's concepts;" "look deep inside yourself, there is infinite wisdom;" and "oneness is the essential realization."[1]

I was astounded, intrigued and, most of all, confused about the source of these statements. I had never consciously experienced such a process before. I was subsequently informed that a channel had been opened to my inner self. In such instances, revelations of wisdom are allowed to flow into one's consciousness. This experience was the origin of my personal exploration of spirituality and the conscious integration of it into my life. It allowed me to reconnect to a dimension of my inner self that I had earlier chosen to shut down. I use this connection as a continuing source of inspiration, wisdom, and guidance for how I live my life.

William A. Guillory

Acknowledgements

To Katie

Acknowledgments

First, and foremost, I acknowledge those individuals who have given me permission to share their stories of personal and spiritual transformation. Some of them chose to be anonymous. Second, I am appreciative to those who have contributed to my growth since I began my journey of spiritual transformation. Third, I am forever grateful to those who have supported and nurtured me personally through the most difficult period of my life: Barbara, Chris, Danny, Katie, and Mutiu; and professionally Don and Lee. Fourth, I acknowledge loved ones who aided in my development from childhood even when I was unaware that I was on a spiritual path. And finally, I am thankful to those individuals who are responsible for the beauty of this text—Tatiana Bagge, Thomas Kotter, and my editors, Chris and Becky Harding.

Foreword

Change is accelerating all around us. Customers' expectations are rising constantly. Employees are expecting real meaning in their work and pride in their employer. The globalization of all segments of the economy grows, and as Guillory points out, embracing globalization by definition means embracing diversity. Our interconnectedness with our environment demands acknowledgment and action.

In The Living Organization—*Spirituality in the Workplace*, Bill Guillory is, once again, exploring critical terrain for organizations that wish to anticipate or, at least, react to these changes and thrive into the 21st Century.

Guillory helps us to individually explore our inner spirit and bring the rest of our lives, including our work lives, into alignment with that spirit. He also helps us to understand why and how spirituality is going to be part of the workplace that high-performing employees are going to expect.

Creating Living Organizations and bringing spirituality into our workplace is firstly a moral issue, but it will also be a competitive necessity in the 21st Century. The ensuing pages push back our blinders to see this more clearly and point us toward the journey ahead.

Jack Lowe
CEO
TDIndustries

Preface

When I first saw the early drafts of this book I was impressed. Bill Guillory masterfully demonstrates the value of congruence on both an individual and organizational level. His examples and anecdotes show the reader how the successful businesses of the future will prosper into the 21st Century. They will do so by creating a greater purpose than themselves and a workplace where passionate and empowered employees experience meaning in their work.

These Living Organizations will create the new leaders of business—individuals who are motivated from within to achieve the organization's business objectives. This New Leadership will inspire others by *living* spiritual values and *modelling* their corresponding principles. They will be naturally driven to both operate profitably and exceed the expectations of customers.

The Living Organizations he describes here serve as models for the companies most likely to succeed in the coming years as we navigate the whitewater of tumultuous change in values, global economics, social responsibility, and worker fulfillment. This book is one of the best works that connects spirituality and successful enterprise. Read and enjoy.

John E. Renesch, Editor
The New Leaders business newsletter;
Leadership in a New Era: Visionary Approaches to the Biggest Crisis of our Times

Contents

Introduction

> "In visionary companies, the drive for
> progress arises from a deep human urge—to
> explore, to create, to change, to improve. It's a
> deep, inner, compulsive—almost primal—drive."

Built to Last
James C. Collins and Jerry I. Porrus

A *Living Organization* is one which re-creates itself in response to the changing internal and external business environment. Internal changes are primarily stimulated by external changes—largely on the part of customer demands and the expanding global marketplace. As Europe, dominated by Germany, and the Far East, dominated by Japan, became formidable economic forces in the 1970s and 1980s, the world's resources began to flow away from the U.S. Inefficiency, both in processes and management systems, could no longer be accommodated for organizations to remain profitable. Thus, the era of reengineering, restructuring, and downsizing was ushered in. Today we find ourselves asking, what is the essential ingredient necessary to ensure the short and long-term success of an organization? This text presents a compelling argument for why spirituality may be that ingredient, when consciously acknowledged and channeled into an organization's day-to-day operation.

Spirituality is the life force that permeates and drives a Living Organization in the pursuit of its business objectives. Spirituality is often confused with religious belief systems. The two are different, although they are related. Spirituality is derived from *inner consciousness*

—beyond systems of belief, whether these systems are taught or learned. Religious belief systems are sourced *from* spirituality. Religion is form and spirituality is the source behind the form. In fact, the spiritual dimension is where all religious belief systems merge into one, without distinction.

Present business pressures for more successful operation are creating new workplace demands. They are forcing us to acknowledge that a radically different way of operating is going to be required for business survival and competitiveness. At the heart of this transformation process is the acknowledgment that *competent people are our only long-term competitive advantage.* Other types of competitive advantages are either temporary or transitory. Therefore, a fundamental premise of this book is, to be creative and innovative in today's workplace requires the whole person—body, mind, and spirit. We must reunite with our spirituality and make it a legitimate part of the working environment.

The systems of operation that have the greatest probability for success in the 21st Century are those that are based upon the belief in the potential of the human spirit. The implementation of these systems begins with the acknowledgment that we have not created work environments where people are given the authority to be responsible and accountable for their work in proportion to their competencies. When provided this opportunity, most individuals respond by tapping into an inherent inner source that drives their performance. Therefore, the most powerful source of motivation comes from within. In fact, this is the *only* sustainable source of motivation. This text is a description of this inner source and how each of us might access it by simply being open and receptive to the ideas and suggestions discussed in this book.

Introduction

Spirituality in the Workplace, this book's subtitle, is the integration of humanistic principles, practices, and behaviors with sound business functioning. These include employee-friendly work environments, service orientation, creativity and innovation, personal and collective transformation, environmental sensitivity, and high performance. The five key elements in integrating spirituality into the workplace are: *people, service, organizational self-awareness, wisdom,* and *the new leadership.*

This text is a detailed accounting of how each of these five elements are interwoven to produce a high-performing organization. The pattern of presentation begins with sound business principles geared toward creating exceptional individual and collective performance. These principles are brought to life by numerous examples to which the reader can relate. The final part of the pattern is a discussion of what might be learned from each example that can serve to empower us in adapting to accelerated change and achieving personal stability. At the end of each chapter, there are exercises and suggestions for implementing the ideas discussed throughout the text.

In the Appendices, there are discussions of: questions people ask about spirituality and the workplace; a self-test to determine how spiritual you are; and the stepwise process of integrating spirituality into your organizational culture. A special feature of this book is that it serves, in part, as a personal adaptation manual for succeeding in a chaotically changing world.

William A. Guillory
September, 1999

Chapter One

The Living Organization— Creatively Adapting to Accelerated Change

"The law of natural selection applies to organizations in today's constantly changing business environment. In other words, those that learn to continually adapt, survive."

The Author

Introduction

A Living Organization is one that continually adapts to its changing business environment. Adaptation occurs as a result of individual and organizational transformation. Transformation is an irreversible change in the mind-set of an organization's leadership and employees that sets the stage for continuous improvement and often a new way of operating. Such change commonly results in an organization redefining its vision, strategy, and performance expectations. An organization's drive to continually change is similar to the adaptive nature of biological organisms that evolve over time. And, as is true for biological organisms, those organizations that do not learn to adapt, usually become extinct.

This chapter will discuss the four Darwinian characteristics of Living Organizations and show that, particularly during crisis, these characteristics are key to an organization's ability to survive and prosper. The chapter will also show how Living Organizations endure over time through *adaptation, empowerment,* and *high performance.*

What Is a Living Organization?

The key characteristic of a Living Organization is its ability to continually transform in response to the changing business environment. For example, in the mid-1980s it became clear to many business leaders that operating an organization according to the previously acceptable "command and control" style was no longer competitive. This way of operating had simply become too slow, inefficient, and resistant to change to keep up with the complexity of accelerated change experienced by most companies. In response to that realization, proactive organizations began the significant integration of high employee involvement, teamwork, and empowerment into their management practices.

For instance, Frank Marchand, the vice president of sales for the Canadian subsidiary of a major U.S. oil conglomerate, found himself faced with declining market share. Frank's parent company had always operated in the traditional hierarchical manner. In spite of the fact that his subsidiary operated in a similar manner, Frank had never really believed that control management was the most effective way to get the best from people. Now, however, faced with declining market share, Frank knew that he had to significantly change his operation.

After considerable thought, Frank decided to make a proposal to the parent company that involved a two-year commitment to the implementation of high employee involvement processes. In preparation for his presentation to the corporation's senior leadership, he developed a comprehensive plan for reducing hierarchy, providing training, and developing sales teams. He also suggested in his proposal that giving employees and sales representatives greater autonomy would not only result in the company regaining its market share, but would also create new business opportunities as well. Although the corporate leadership was not totally comfortable with the new management philosophy Frank was recommending, they accepted his proposal anyway—primarily because of his outstanding record of success in sales.

Frank was excited about the approval of his proposal. The implementation of his plan began with a comprehensive 360° Executive Assessment. As it turned out, an important result of the assessment was that many of Frank's senior managers were surprised by the employee feedback they received. They were unaware of the counterproductive impact their management style had on the attitude and performance of their employees.

Another crucial part of the assessment was a one-on-one facilitation provided by an external consultant who addressed interpersonal issues that had been identified by the employee feedback. Each executive was then responsible for creating a plan to resolve these interpersonal issues, in addition to any performance issues that may have been identified. Frank's division immediately began implementing the various executive plans supported by the new high involvement management style. Not surprisingly, the receptivity to Frank's program was very positive. During the first year, sales, morale, and overall performance increased dramatically. By the end of the second year, his organization exceeded their sales goals.

Eventually, Frank's mode of operation began to cause a strain between himself and the corporate president of sales. This conflict was probably inevitable since their basic philosophies of management were diametrically different. Frank favored high employee involvement while the corporate president in the U.S. favored a more hierarchical style. As the president gradually imposed more severe restrictions on Frank's operation, his organization's sales started to decline. Key managers who believed in Frank's way of running the business began to leave, further accelerating the decline of the operation. When it became clear that this dilemma was unresolvable, Frank resigned.

From a long-term perspective, this story would appear to be an example of how adaptation did not work. But Frank conveyed to me an important realization in retrospect. "The real value of what we accomplished in those two years was the degree of personal and professional growth realized by each individual in the organization," he said. In fact, one of the statements Frank made in his resignation speech to his employees was, "You people are empowered, so I'm not worried. You can look after yourselves." It is worth noting that the employees who did leave were able to get significant positions in other organizations throughout the world. The growth and self-confidence they acquired under Frank's program far exceeded what they had accomplished when managed by the hierarchical system that previously existed.

Frank later recounted that he had experienced a major realization about himself during his own one-on-one facilitation. He had begun to view himself as being driven by a purpose greater than simply meeting and exceeding sales goals. Indeed, he discovered that his overriding objective was to create an environment where his employees had the opportunity to become fully functional, capable, and self-confident individuals. Since he had clearly accomplished *this* objective, Frank considers the two-year program a huge success.

Frank Marchand also learned that his natural desire to facilitate the empowerment of others originated from an inner dimension of himself that he describes as spiritual. Through this experience he also came to realize that "spirituality" is probably the source that inspires most of us to live consistent with our life purpose.

The prevailing question that drives the evolution of a Living Organization, is the same question that Frank had asked himself in response to his company's declining market share, which is: "How do we continually adapt to accelerated change?" If the answers to that question reveal outdated processes, products, or services within one's organization, then significant changes may be appropriate or necessary. Quite often, as Frank's example demonstrates, the changes required may result in both personal and collective transformation while simultaneously achieving the organization's business objectives.

Perhaps the greatest phenomenon impacting organizational change and adaptation are the advancements in information technology. These advancements have revolutionized business marketing (on-line sales), communication (E-mail), and the delivery of consulting services (computer-assisted learning). A specific illustration of how empowerment and information technology transformed the delivery of one company's consulting services is presented in the following case study.

Innovations International—How Do We Make Ourselves Desirable but Unnecessary?

In 1994, Innovations International, a well-established consulting firm, decided to reinvent itself. After reviewing some of its ongoing research, the company's leadership reached the conclusion that the education and training market was going to be significantly affected by the development of new information technology. Some of the major benefits for clients who receive organizational education and training included: reduced costs, greater flexibility, decentralization, and greater control for employees. These factors led Innovations to reassess their philosophy of delivering training products and services and prompted the company leadership to ask the following questions:

1) How necessary are external consultants for an effective training process to occur?

2) Can in-house consultants and line managers deliver training as effectively as outside experts?

3) What if we designed our training and development programs to *ensure* our customers' success?

The responses to these questions forced the Innovations team to realize that in-house people are just as capable as external consultants in delivering a creatively designed, "user-friendly" program; and, because of their personal experiences, in-house people are often more credible.

Prompted by the responses to the questions above, the team then asked themselves an even more challenging question:

4) How does a consulting firm design programs to make its own external consultants unnecessary?

Upon seriously considering this fundamental issue, the team came to the conclusion that any mature seminar program can be converted into a self-paced product, such as a video program or computer-assisted learning (CAL) program. Through additional research and more in-depth experimentation, the company also learned that CALs can be effectively used either as a single-user or group-user program. Perhaps even more importantly for their clients, however, the Innovations team also confirmed that this approach could indeed be effectively implemented by in-house personnel and line managers —as long as they were properly trained.

Today, Innovations is a growing product-oriented company that is based upon a permanent foundation of new innovative seminars, measurement instruments, and consulting services. In response to the changing business climate, the company altered its approach to seminar design and presentation from customer dependency to customer empowerment. Consistent with their change in business focus, Innovations created a new strategic plan—one that is not set in stone, but instead is constantly changing as the company receives market and customer feedback. An organization's ability to be agile and flexible in response to change is an example of how the adaptation process successfully plays out in business. This case study demonstrates the very essence of *creative adaptation*—the willingness to question the most fundamental assumptions about one's business operations, *in anticipation of change!*

The Essence of Adaptation

As illustrated by the Innovations case study, the essence of adaptation is based upon continually asking oneself the following questions with respect to the business market:

1) Who are we?

2) Why do we exist?

3) What is our defining character or heritage?

4) What is our vision?

5) How do we express our vision (in products or services)?

6) Who is our customer?

7) How do we market and sell our products and services most effectively?

8) How do we exceed our customers' expectations?

9) What is our most productive system of operation?

10) How do we care for our people?

11) How do we integrate humanistic practices with sound business functioning?

Brainstorming these questions on a regular basis is an excellent way to keep pace with change—or to even anticipate it. The regular application of this process can also prevent the necessity of adaptation driven by crisis.

Notable examples of organizational adaptation due to necessity that occurred in the 1990s are IBM and Eastman Kodak. IBM underwent a change in leadership, a redefinition of the corporation, and the creation of a new business strategy in 1993. This change was principally triggered by a decline in market share and profitability that was approaching the critical point. The most dramatic internal adjustment required was their transformation from a traditional, slow-response culture, to one focused on speed and service. Although IBM was again profitable by 1996, it should not go unnoticed that a critical part of their strategy included the elimination of 35,000 jobs. Now, however, after having changed the mind-set and business practices of the corporation, IBM is again a leader in its field.

Eastman Kodak provides a less traumatic example of adaptation that occurred when the company changed its leadership in 1994. At that time, George Fisher, formerly President and CEO of Motorola, stepped in to run the company. Concurrent with this change in leadership, Kodak redefined its mission in response to the rapidly changing global environment. The new mission statement, as shown on the following page, is an example of a company's commitment to excellence in response to accelerated change.

Eastman Kodak Company's Mission

"We will build a world-class results-oriented culture based on our five values; Respect for the Individual, Uncompromising Integrity, Trust, Credibility, and Continuous Improvement and Personal Renewal through which we will grow more rapidly than our competitors by providing customers and consumers with solutions they want to capture, store, process, output, and communicate images to people and machines anywhere, anytime. We will derive our competitive advantage by bringing differentiated, cost-effective solutions—including consumables, hardware, software, systems, and services— to the marketplace quickly and with flawless quality through a diverse team of energetic employees with the world-class talent and skills necessary to sustain Kodak as the World Leader in Imaging. In this way, we will achieve our fundamental objective of Total Customer Satisfaction and our consequent goals of Increased Global Market Share and Superior Financial Performance."

Change or Die!

Unfortunately, the greatest impetus to change for most organizations is necessity. Whether it is a crisis or more traumatically, the "burning platform," the reality of today's world is: "change or go out of business." Measurable business indicators that signal crisis or sound the alarm in regard to the "burning platform" are: decline in market share, revenues, productivity, employee morale, and quality of work life. Most of all, the decline of a business is due to a lack of visionary leadership.

Organizations that are more prone to experience the indicators listed above are those that have had exclusive services, monopolies, or patented products. Examples include communications services and public utilities, as well as government agencies and subsidies. In essence, these organizations have operated uncompetitively for years. And although a company may intellectually prepare for the loss of an exclusive service or a patent, the reality of such a loss is usually more traumatic than anticipated. This is particularly true when an organization loses its market share to competing organizations. This loss of subsidized revenue or market share is commonly due to a lack of financial accountability or the undercutting of established prices by the competition. When faced with these kinds of challenges, adaptive organizations renew their sense of commitment and dedication. They adopt a willingness to change driven by a desire to survive and prosper.

The recent challenge faced by The National Scientific Laboratories is an illustration of how these government supported agencies adapted to such a situation. The Laboratories are principally funded by the Departments of Defense, Energy, and Commerce. When funds normally available to operate these research facilities were cut, they were faced with a crisis. A major transformation in their mind-set was necessary for their continued existence. This transformation involved the realization that while basic research was necessary, it was no longer sufficient, on its own, to justify year-to-year funding. It was also necessary for the laboratories to generate products and services of value to their "subsidizers," the taxpayers. As a result, an additional mission was established by the federal government. It is "to enhance America's industrial effectiveness by performing research for useful civilian applications."

In response to the new mission, The Oak Ridge, Tennessee, National Laboratory (called X-10), in collaboration with local Knoxville hospitals, discovered a 99%-accurate laser technique for detecting colon cancer. The previous procedure required an intrusive surgical operation. In a like manner, the Laboratory's support staff was challenged with operating more productively with fewer resources. They were also required to learn a customer service attitude much like that of the profit-driven business world. The consequence of not adopting these changes in performance and attitude, in a relatively short time frame, was downsizing. Unfortunately, in this case, downsizing occurred in spite of their efforts.

The successful adaptation of the Oak Ridge facility and most of the other National Laboratories in response to decreased funding is a classic example of how resilient and talented people ·can be when they are committed, dedicated, and willing to change.

The stories of IBM, Kodak, and The National Scientific Laboratories reveal critical characteristics that Living Organizations tap into when faced with either survival or adaptation. These characteristics are synonymous with the four Darwinian principles of living systems discussed in the following section.

The Four Darwinian Principles of Living Systems— Characteristics for Adaptation

Like biological systems, change within a business environment is driven by an innate consciousness for adaptation. The principles of adaptation for Living Organizations are strikingly similar in operation to the four Darwinian principles of living systems. Within a specific living (or business) system:

1. *All species display natural variation.* Businesses selling the same products or services have distinct differences. For automobile manufacturers, examples of this principle would include Lexus, Infinity, BMW, Chrysler Concorde, and Cadillac Deville. Other industries with their own similar comparisons are airlines, computer manufacturers, software developers, healthcare providers, and public utilities.

2. *The number of offspring produced far exceed the number that will survive into adulthood.* In general, eighty percent of all new businesses are unsuccessful. More than fifty percent of the Fortune 500 companies from twenty years ago do not exist today.

3. *Some offspring are better at adapting to their habitat (business environment) than others.* Examples include: Boeing, Toyota, Compaq, Microsoft, Primary Children's Medical Center of Salt Lake, and Texas Utilities Electric of Dallas, Texas.

4. *The better-adapted organisms transmit part of their adaptation characteristics to their offspring.*

These transmitted characteristics become the defining character or philosophy that evolves within an organization and endures over time.

Using these principles as a template for successful adaptation, the four characteristics that follow from each of the statements above are: *uniqueness, perseverance, acclimation,* and *heritage.* These are exemplified below for various types of organizations.

Uniqueness—a distinguishing quality that separates an organization from similar-looking competitors. For example, each of the companies listed below distinguish themselves within their respective industries as follows:

Boeing — "Leading-edge pioneers in aircraft design"

Toyota — "High quality, low-repair automobiles"

Hewlett Packard — "Innovation"

Microsoft — "User-friendly software"

Apple Computer — "User-friendly computers"

Primary Children's Medical Center — "The child first and always"

Perseverance—the will to succeed, no matter what difficulties or obstacles are encountered. For example:

Boeing is succeeding in spite of increasing competition from global aircraft producers.

Toyota succeeds in spite of high import charges leading to increased sticker prices.

Hewlett Packard is streamlining production and inventory of high-demand printers.

Microsoft continues to produce quality performing products in mass demand.

Apple Computer is persisting and succeeding while competing in a dominant personal computer world.

Primary Children's Medical Center is maintaining quality service while experiencing steadily increasing costs.

Acclimation—an ability to continually adapt and contribute to the changing business system. Some examples of acclimation are:

Boeing designs and produces the next generation aircraft to serve a specific market need.

Toyota increases quality, lowers repairs, and maintains high trade-in value.

Hewlett Packard continues to lead in the laser printer field and in new innovation.

Microsoft introduces Windows 98 and NT.

Apple Computer creates new leadership, a new strategy, focused products/markets, and new partnerships.

Primary Children's Medical Center reengineers the total hospital operation.

Heritage—a defining character or philosophy that is synonymous with an organization's people, products, and services, and subsequently passed to succeeding generations:

> Boeing — "The acknowledged leader in aviation"

> Toyota — "Exceptional quality automobiles and customer service," *"The relentless pursuit of perfection"*

> Hewlett Packard — "Creativity and innovation"

> Microsoft — "Aggressive mass market penetration"

> Apple Computer — "Leading-edge computer and software innovations"

> Primary Children's Medical Center — "Compassion for children"

These four characteristics of Living Organizations ensure their adaptability over time. They are such an ingrained part of their respective cultures that they are rarely, if ever, questioned.

Living Organizations Are Empowered

Although Living Organizations do experience the "ups and downs" of the business cycle, they are *profitable*, *productive*, and *employee-supportive* over time. These three criteria define an empowered organization.[2] Each of these criterion is specific, definable, and measurable, and is discussed in turn below.

A profitable organization produces more value-added products and services than the capital necessary to operate that organization. Living Organizations experience an interesting dilemma with respect to profit-ability. On one hand, profitability is a requirement for survival and, on the other, survival is often dependent on promoting the success of other companies through partnerships. An example of how this dilemma can be resolved is demonstrated by the experience of Lester Washington, President and CEO of Engineering Dynamics.

Lester, an African-American male, earned his under-graduate degree in electrical engineering from Howard University and a graduate degree from the Harvard Business School. Upon graduation from Harvard, Lester started his own company that served as a manufacturing supplier. He quickly realized that his company's long-term success was dependent upon networking with other similar or competitive companies, as well as those he sought to serve. As his company struggled through the first two years, it was kept solvent by network leads and recommendations. When the diversity effort of a major photographic company began to emphasize part-nerships with small minority-owned businesses, Lester was able to secure a major strategic alliance as a sole provider. This partnership agreement involved a five-year contract.

Based on his company's exceptional service, the photographic company suggested that Lester expand into a new engineering area required by their operation. They offered to assist Lester's company in becoming expert in this area as part of their strategic alliance. Lester was excited about the offer to expand his com-pany and the profits that would result. However, upon reflection, he remembered that a person who was a member of his network group was already expert in the new engineering area. Lester was faced with a dilemma:

accept the new opportunity in his own self-interest or recommend a member of the network who was already expert and successful. Also involved was the ethical issue of giving back to the network for the support he received during the first two years of his business.

After serious soul-searching, Lester recommended his network colleague to the photographic company. He felt this decision was in the best interest of his integrity and the network that had sustained him during the difficult times. The photographic company informed Lester that their offer was based upon an interest in expanding minority-owned business opportunities with their company. His network partner was a white male. Still, Lester refused to take the offer and informed his network partner of the business opportunity.

What Lester did not know was that this particular individual had highly recommended him for the original contract he had been awarded by the photographic company. When the photographic company, Lester, and his network colleague came together to resolve the impasse, it was agreed that Lester *and* his network colleague should form a partnership involving the new engineering project. Thus, with his network partner's expertise, Lester did not require the assistance of the photographic company in developing expertise in this new area of engineering. As a result, Lester and his company acquired the working knowledge of a new technical area and gained an external partnership that would allow them to expand far beyond what might have come about if he had accepted the original offer.

This example is not meant to suggest that an organization should sacrifice profitability to the detriment of their employees and shareholders. However, the overriding driving force of successful organizations is to operate in a manner that best serves the customer. In this particular case, it was not necessary to "reinvent the wheel." In other words, the expertise Lester needed already existed. This situation also provided the opportunity for Lester to test his own integrity in terms of supporting the success of others. This supportive, integrity-based mind-set is only possible where scarcity and greed do not exist. Most of all, it is based upon the absence of fear. When fear is absent, spirituality is present.

A productive organization generates its products and services in the most cost-effective manner possible. To do so, the organization must continually be improving its processes, products, and services so that profitability is created *before* these products and services are sold to customers. An interesting illustration of this empowerment criterion is the example of a major aircraft corporation that acquired a contract in 1996 from an air transport consortium. The contract involved the production of 150 airplanes over a six-year period. The company knew before going into this agreement that if they stuck with their then-present production processes, they would lose money on the project. The executive management determined that over the entire six-year period of the contract their internal production processes, such as cycle time, etc., would measurably increase in efficiency. Increased efficiency is synonymous with lower production costs. Thus, over the duration of the project, the company would realize a significant profit. In this sense, *productive* is synonymous with continuous quality improvement.

An employee-supportive organization provides *all* employees unlimited opportunity for professional development, advancement, and quality of work life. It is also sensitive to the needs of employees when family or work life situations require unusual working arrangements in order to retain a valued employee. An example of such sensitivity is illustrated by Jill Sorensen's story.

Jill worked for a small retail business in the Midwest. The president, Don Stevens, always believed that his employees were progressive in their thinking. However, when Jill became pregnant, rumors were rampant in the company that she would not return. Since she joined the organization, Jill had been a fast riser. Don had invested considerable time and money in her development. He had always assumed she would be a career employee rather than someone simply filling a job. When Jill informed him that her family came first and that she had decided to leave the company until her baby was two or three years old, Don was faced with an unpleasant dilemma.

Don decided that he couldn't let someone as talented and valuable as Jill simply walk away. So he offered her an opportunity to work five to ten hours a week, once she had sufficiently recovered from her childbirth experience. Surprised by how much she was valued, Jill accepted Don's offer. Two years after her baby was born, Jill had begun to increase her work schedule. Her productivity and management skills also grew steadily. Shortly after her child turned seven, Jill became vice president of operations and began to handle the day-to-day operations of the entire organization.

This success story illustrates what it means to be employee-supportive, especially when outdated beliefs and attitudes surface that could lead to the loss of a potentially valuable employee. In this case, it was recognizing that childbearing is a natural part of the family process and that it should be accommodated as part of an employee's work cycle.

This example also shows how a growing number of empowered organizations are responding to family and worklife situations in order to retain highly competent employees. In a rapidly changing business world, they realize that their organization's future depends on their ability to be flexible, adaptable, and creative in response to the changing needs of the work force. *Profitability, productivity,* and *employee-supportiveness* are the result of practicing and institutionalizing the phrase, *people are our most important resource.*

Living Organizations Are High Performing

As living systems transform from generation to generation, they are in a continuing process of becoming high performing. High performance is the process of maximizing the synergy of a system's components. In a like manner, the objective of an organization is to become high performing and maintain that level of performance over time. Therefore, a high-performance organization is one that continually leverages the total capacity of its people in achieving its business (or organizational) objectives. It integrates initiatives such as Teamwork, Quality, Work Process Redesign, Environment, Safety and Health, Customer Focus, Diversity, and Empowerment into its day-to-day operation as shown in Figure 1 on the following page.

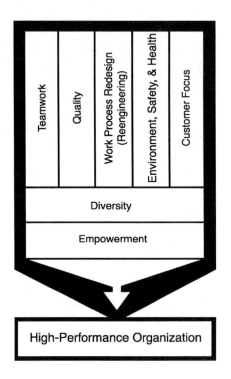

Figure 1.   Diagram of a high-performance organization

The initiatives depicted vertically in Figure 1 are well-defined processes and systems. Each of these is uniquely designed for a given organization. For example, many organizations have implemented their quality initiative based upon the principles and practices of Total Quality Management (TQM). Diversity is the "people factor" and determines how effectively each of the vertical initiatives is implemented—either alone or in combinations. For example, if a cross-functional team is created for improved customer service, such as DaimlerChrysler platform teams, they automatically integrate the principles and practices learned from their quality initiative. If necessary, they may also institute new reengineered team processes based upon fewer steps as well as the extensive utilization of information technology. Implementation is either enhanced or limited in performance depending on how effectively diversity differences are resolved. These differences include how people are (*human diversity*), how people think (*cultural diversity*), and how they prefer to do things (*systems diversity*).

Empowerment is common to all of the vertical initiatives in terms of how they are all implemented—high employee involvement. This means that the team is delegated greater authority, within specific guidelines, to produce the team's objectives. Leadership operates in a more strategic manner in setting the context, guidelines, and goals to be achieved. The team and leadership also jointly establish accountability measures that must be achieved during the process in order to continually *earn* the freedom of unmanaged operation.

High Performance Is Spiritually Driven

One organization that exemplifies spiritually-driven high performance is TDIndustries of Dallas, Texas. When this construction firm was faced with going out of business in 1989, its president and CEO, Jack Lowe Jr., was challenged to call upon both his inner strength and the defining philosophy that characterized the organization since its inception: "Our people are our strength." It was Jack's father who started this family-owned business in 1946 and institutionalized humanistic values into its operation. He had also been very active in the integration of the Dallas public school system. Thus, TDIndustries and its philosophy was more than just a business to Jack Lowe Jr., it was his family's legacy.

At the height of their crisis in 1989, Jack shares that he came to the realization that if the organization was to survive, it would be through the shared leadership of the various business leaders. Each of them would have to examine the depth of their commitment to reversing the trend toward bankruptcy. Jack, along with others, invested his lifetime savings as an example of his faith and commitment to the organization's success. In addition, TDIndustries employees were offered stock in the company in exchange for their retirement funds in order for the company to secure the necessary working capital during this turbulent period. Jack asked each of the business leaders to come up with plans for how their business units could more effectively respond to the radical changes occurring in the construction industry. In response, they each created aggressive plans for reinventing their respective business unit. Gradually, they began reversing the downward trend and in three to four years, they were profitable again. Throughout this crisis period, they never compromised their enduring values based on spiritual principles.

In 1998, TDIndustries experienced its most prosperous year. The organization's profits were the highest in its history. Of equal importance, the annual employee satisfaction survey was 93% positive. Most of all, the differential between ethnic minorities and majority employees closed to just 1%, whereas two years earlier it had been 10%. During that two-year period, Jack had been a relentless advocate of diversity for ethnic minorities and women. Although TDIndustries is performing in an exceptional manner at present, the challenge for them will be to continue in this manner, especially in a world of increasing complexity, ambiguity, and accelerated change.

Jack actively promotes the servant-leader philosophy of the Robert K. Greenleaf Foundation:[3] "A servant-leader is a person who begins with a natural feeling of wanting to serve *first*—to help, support, encourage and lift up others. And because of his or her role model, others begin to lead by serving."

What we learn from this example is that success and spiritual values are compatible. In fact, spiritual values are often the source of an organization's ability to adapt effectively to change, particularly during difficulty or crisis. Unfortunately, adaptation is too often motivated by survival; and a survival mentality promotes short-term, adversarial behavior. On the other hand, adaptation based upon enduring spiritual values promotes behavior that is truly beneficial to customers, the organization, and the business system.

How might you discover if your organization is adaptive, empowered, *and* high performing? Apply the measurement instruments shown on the following pages to you and your organization.

Empowerment and High Performance Measurements

Apply the measurement instruments shown below, and those on the following pages, to your organization. These assessments can be used to determine how personally empowered (competent) your employees are, how supportive your organization's leadership support system is, and whether you presently have a high-performance organization. Respond to each question below as: Strongly Agree (SA); Agree (A); Neutral (N); Disagree (D); or Strongly Disagree (SD).

Number	Statement	Choice
1	I am *totally* responsible for my success at work.	
2	I am exceptionally productive, irrespective of the work environment.	
3	I am accountable for the results I produce, even if a situation is unfair.	
4	I practice continuous learning to upgrade my skills and competencies on a *regular* basis, without the necessity of being told.	
5	I am exceptionally skilled for the work (or job) I do as *demonstrated by my performance.*	
6	I trust co-workers (or associates) without interference, when I delegate tasks vital *to my own success.*	
7	I have demonstrated exceptional interpersonal skills where mentorship or coaching is concerned.	
8	I hold co-workers (or associates) to their commitments, even when it provokes confrontation.	
9	I hold others proactively accountable for their commitments, regardless of how it may affect our personal relationship.	
10	I am willing to work through in-depth personal issues in order to achieve team success.	

Personal Empowerment Assessment Evaluation

For each of the responses on the previous page, follow the instructions below to obtain a numerical score.

Number of SA responses _____ x 4.0 = _____

A responses _____ x 3.0 = _____

N responses _____ x 2.0 = _____

D responses _____ x 1.0 = _____

SD responses _____ x 0.0 = _____

Total = _____

Multiply the total by 2.5 to obtain your total percentage of Personal Empowerment based upon a 100% scale.

Total _____ x 2.5 = _____%

The average score of individuals taking this assessment is 77%.

Leadership Support System Assessment

Answer each of the following questions on the basis of your perceptions or experiences of how your organization operates: Strongly Agree (SA); Agree (A); Neutral (N); Disagree (D); Strongly Disagree (SD). As you respond to each of the statements, use your organization's unique definition of leadership.

Number	Statement	Choice
1	This organization fully utilizes its employees (or associates).	
2	This organization values its employees (or associates).	
3	This organization provides me with training opportunities for my professional growth.	
4	This organization makes it clear that it values empowerment.	
5	This organization values and rewards teamwork.	
6	Job assignments are based on who needs opportunities for growth and development.	
7	Non-confidential information is freely distributed in this organization.	
8	I am provided timely feedback on my job performance.	
9	The leadership of this organization inspires employees (or associates) by being examples of what they expect.	
10	Where employees (or associates) are affected, leadership includes them in planning/implementing.	

Leadership Support System Evaluation

For each of the responses on the previous page, follow the instructions below to obtain a numerical score.

Number of SA responses_____ x 4.0 = _____
A responses_____ x 3.0 = _____
N responses_____ x 2.0 = _____
D responses_____ x 1.0 = _____
SD responses_____ x 0.0 = _____

Total _____

Multiply the total by 2.5 to obtain your total percentage of the Leadership Support System based upon a 100% scale.

Total _____ x 2.5 = _____%

The average score of organizations taking this assessment is 65%.

Conclusions

1. If your Personal Empowerment Assessment percentage is greater than the Leadership Support System percentage, then leadership is not delegating sufficient authority in proportion to your competence.

2. If your Personal Empowerment Assessment percentage is less than the Leadership Support System percentage, then you need to become more personally empowered— that is, to create and execute a plan for becoming more competent in specific areas relating to your performance.

3. If your Personal Empowerment Assessment percentage is about equal (±2%) to the Leadership Support System percentage, then you might use the model below for becoming more empowered as an organization in incremental steps based on your "stretch" projects.

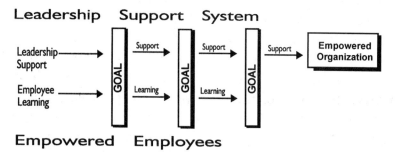

The overall empowerment of your organization is measured by averaging the sum of the Personal Empowerment Assessment and the Leadership Support System Assessment percentages. If this average is less than 85%, the organization is not yet a high-performance organization.

Chapter Two

Spirituality—The Source of Wisdom

*"Spirituality is the infinite reservoir of wisdom.
Each human life is a channel through which
that divine wisdom is steadily flowing."*

Paramahansa Yogananda

Introduction

We are so busy living life that we rarely stop to ask ourselves, "Where do we get the energy to succeed at work in spite of the overwhelming pressures we face?" It seems that most of us are experiencing increased demands for greater productivity in shorter time frames. For example, Joyce Newcomb was recently promoted to vice president of sales at a large pharmaceutical company. Because of new competitive technology in her industry, the time frame for dominating that market has changed from one year to six months. Therefore, Joyce is now expected to accomplish in four months what her business unit used to achieve in six months only a year ago. These new and more demanding expectations are part of the sales strategy employed by Joyce's company in connection with a new "breakthrough drug" that they are bringing to market. Hence, *time* becomes the critical factor in Joyce maximizing profitability for her company.

In spite of the fact that Joyce was successful in meeting her sales goals, she still has anxiety about being able to continually perform under such pressures.

The solution to adjusting to the increasing demands of the changing workplace is *creative adaptation*. Creative adaptation is learning how to consciously tap into an internal source of inspiration and creativity—inspiration to assure us that we can achieve the task at hand and creativity to assist us in coming up with an innovative, successful solution. This process of looking inward and exploring for answers beyond our self-imposed limitations is sometimes referred to as "getting out of the box." Beyond the box of our ordinary limited way of thinking is an inner source that is spiritual. It was from this inner spiritual source that Joyce found the answer to her sales challenge.

In this chapter, we will define spirituality and show how you and your organization can benefit from its incorporation by:

- Listening to that small inner voice

- Learning to adapt to new workplace demands

- Transforming from entitlement to empowerment

- Integrating ethics and values with workplace operations

- Instituting moral responsibility

- Accepting social responsibility

- Shifting from competition to cooperation

What Is Spirituality?

Spirituality is our inner consciousness. It is the source of inspiration, creativity, and wisdom. That which is spiritual comes from within—beyond our *programmed* beliefs and values. Programmed beliefs and values are those that we have been taught, but that have not been tested by challenging life experiences. For example, empowerment is a test of whether we truly believe that job security is based upon performance or entitlement. The challenge is whether we believe we continually *earn* a job through performance or we are *owed* a job because of loyalty. In the past, we have been programmed to believe that we were owed a job because of long-term loyalty.

Spirituality and religion are often thought to be the same, but in fact, they are different. Spirituality is a way of being that predetermines how we respond to life experiences; whereas, religion deals with the incorporation and implementation of organized belief systems. Religion is actually *a* form that spirituality takes in practice. Spirituality is the source behind the form. Spirituality may also be expressed as meditation, Yoga, T'ai Chi, prayer, empathy, compassion, and by treating others with dignity and respect.

Accessing your spirituality involves asking questions (outside of the box) and looking to your inner self for answers. Such a process can be very frustrating initially, since we are rarely encouraged to look within for answers. In general, we have been taught by our culture that the most powerful solutions to our difficulties are provided by outside sources. Spirituality, on the other hand, suggests that the most powerful solutions to our difficulties are within us. In order to fully utilize this innate ability, however, we must develop the skill of learning to look within. This means trusting our intuition when we receive answers that "feel right" but initially do not appear to "make sense."

By way of a personal example, in the early 1980s, I decided to change careers from university professor in physical chemistry to business consultant. It appeared at the time that the "most obvious" route of preparation for my new career was a course of study in business. Upon introspection, a voice within me said, "What you want to introduce into business cannot be achieved by an academic program. It must be acquired through your own personal transformation and then applied to the business world." It took me several days to process this message. The process involved reconciling the intuitive message with its practical implementation. For me, implementation ultimately led to several years of personal transformation, as well as experiencing numerous cultures around the world.

At the time, everyone thought I was crazy since I had been quite successful as a physical chemist. According to conventional wisdom, I probably was crazy. In spite of the dire warnings of many of my colleagues, I resigned my tenured position in the chemistry department and created the consulting company, Innovations International. Trusting the message from my inner self is an indication of how spirituality has become a natural part of my life. For Innovations, spirituality has been a continuing source of our success as a consulting firm for more than 15 years.

TDIndustries—A Case Study

An excellent illustration of how spirituality can shape and influence the workplace is our previously cited example of Jack Lowe Jr., CEO of TDIndustries of Dallas, Texas. Jack inspires his multicultural workforce by declaring, "We must embrace diversity, first and foremost, because it is right." This declaration comes from an inner source that naturally drives *Jack's* commitment to diversity. For those not yet driven by this inner source, he also explains the business necessities and advantages of diversity. However, Jack makes it clear that treating people with dignity and respect is a condition for employment at TDIndustries. Measurements of mind-set, behavior, and goals are made to confirm the meaningful implementation of diversity within the organization. Where there is a *serious* effort in diversity, there is a corresponding spiritually driven leader in terms of human equality. Jack is an example of the kind of individual who is sufficiently in touch with the spiritual dimension of himself that it plays out in practically every aspect of his life.

It is no surprise that this Texas-based construction company was selected 5th in 1998 and 2nd in 1999 by *Fortune* magazine on its list of *The 100 Best Companies to Work for in America.* TDIndustries was also selected in 1995 as Commercial Contractor of the Year by *Contracting Business* magazine. In 1996, they received the Crystal Vision Award from the National Association of Women in Construction for actively promoting growth and opportunities for women in the construction industry. During the same year, Jack was selected to receive the Associated Building Contractor of the Year award, which is usually awarded to an individual. However, upon Jack's request, it was awarded to the TDPartners—the entire employee-owned organization. In 1998, TDIndustries was awarded the Texas Quality Award.

The point is, an organization operates in the most efficient manner when spirituality, in terms of principles and practices, becomes an integrated part of sound business functioning. This is precisely the reason TDIndustries had its most profitable year in 1998 and continues to earn national business awards.

Listening to That Small Inner Voice

The workplace will continue to change at an accelerated rate as we move into the 21st Century. High performance, in terms of increased productivity, will also continue to expand beyond today's expectations. Whatever the product or service, it must be produced faster, cheaper, and better *and* it must exceed the expectations of customers.

In this new emerging work environment, most workers have more to do in less time. The pressure is even greater in organizations where the work force has been downsized while simultaneously creating more ambitious monetary goals. This means that the output per employee must be significantly greater than before downsizing. In other words, there must be a dramatic transformation in each employee's performance. The good news is that we are perfectly capable of such a transformation. The challenging news is that this transformation must be accomplished in increasingly shorter periods of time than we have previously had for such change initiatives.

When faced with changes of this proportion, we begin to examine not only our jobs, but our entire lives. We begin to ask ourselves questions about the meaningfulness of our work. We reexamine the importance of balancing time at work and time with family. Sooner or later, we come to the conclusion that the only meaningful answers to these questions will come from within ourselves. This is the first step of a consciously planned spiritual journey. From this point on, if we choose to consciously continue on this journey, we gain a trust in our inner wisdom that we never experienced before. Sometimes, we discover that much of our life has been lived in a dependent fashion that discouraged the full expression of this inner source. When it is awakened however, possibly through workplace crisis, we often discover a willingness to risk that we never knew existed. The story of Sue Hamilton illustrates this point.

Sue Hamilton is a single mother with two children who worked as a human resource specialist for a large telecommunications company for ten years. Due to reorganization and downsizing, Sue was asked to relocate from San Francisco, where her family and former husband resided, to the Midwest. Sue had been very dedicated and loyal to the company throughout her 10-year employment. As a result, when she was asked to transfer, Sue felt that an important support system in which she had placed her faith, had abandoned her. After working through a period of denial and anger, Sue came to the conclusion that she must do what was best for herself and her children. By her own account, this period involved in-depth personal introspection to discover her passion for work and inner exploration for its expression.

Instead of moving as the organization had requested, Sue decided to leave the company and start her own business as an independent consultant. Her former company provided her a severance package that supported Sue and her family for six months. After launching her company, Sue was able to secure several consulting contracts that provided the opportunity for long-term income. The contracts also involved challenging retraining requirements that Sue had not had in her previous work. These new opportunities invigorated her enthusiasm and thirst for new learning. As an added advantage, Sue now has greater flexibility in arranging her schedule to spend time with her children.

From this story we can see that sometimes what appears to be a crisis is actually an opportunity in disguise. By turning inward and listening to that small inner voice, we find that the answers we need are always there. Once we experience this type of transformation, we can never be the same again. It is like walking through a doorway to our inner wisdom that disappears behind us the instant we enter.

The New Workplace Demands Spirituality

The previous section implies that spirituality is something we must voluntarily choose to tap into as a resource. This statement raises some interesting questions. Given the apparent value of spirituality, why is it not more visibly prevalent in the workplace? Furthermore, setting aside what we may feel to be the obligations of leadership, why don't we, individually, choose to call upon this inner source? And, is the necessity of spirituality eventually inevitable? Answers to these questions can be found in the following story.

Marjorie Stapleton was married with two children and had worked for a major healthcare corporation for fifteen years. She joined the company in her mid-twenties, but as she became more successful at work, she experienced increasing conflict in her home life. By way of background, Marjorie was raised in a traditional nuclear family structure where a wife's career was secondary to a husband's career. In fact, according to this traditional viewpoint, a wife was not supposed to have a career, but simply a job (and then only if it was convenient for the family). Therefore, when Marjorie married, she was expected to maintain the necessary domestic responsibilities, in addition to her job.

Marjorie's success at work began to transform her job into a career. A major source of her success was her ability to manage a variety of employee personalities. This was a skill that Marjorie had acquired as a result of her own process of personal development. As her responsibilities expanded, she began drawing more upon what she described as her "inner strength." For Marjorie, this connection to her inner self was made through daily morning meditations. By *listening to* and *following* her own inner voice, Marjorie began to redefine herself, her professional aspirations, and her family relationships.

Her situation came to a head when it appeared that she was confronted with choosing between family and career. This personal crisis led to a series of gut-wrenching discussions with her spouse that literally threatened their marital relationship. Fortunately, Marjorie was married to someone who realized that if the marriage was to survive, major adjustments would be required of him. After going through intense discussions together, Marjorie and her husband jointly agreed to redefine their marital contract, in practice, to support Marjorie's career aspirations. As a couple, they discovered that the key to maintaining a successful marriage and adjusting to personal workplace is continually focusing on *what works* for both partners.

Marjorie's personal crisis may be unique, but the theme is common. When the aspirations of one partner change in a fundamental way, a relationship requires a major adjustment on the part of the other in order to survive. In dealing with situations of this nature, we are often required to seek solutions that go beyond our traditional beliefs and values that may have little relevance in today's world. Such exploration requires a level of courage that we may not have been previously forced to use. The conclusion we may come to is that the choice to ignore spiritual exploration is fast disappearing. Both workplace and changing societal values will continue to precipitate situations and crises that require "inner space" solutions.

Case in point, in 1999 we considered the impeachment of a U.S. President, not on the basis of his performance or even his having technically broken the law. Instead, the thrust of the impeachment movement was largely based on what many felt to be a lack of moral character on the part of the President—a quality which is spiritual in context. So, whether it is young people seeking spiritual answers; mystical fireflies on a Nissan commercial; Buddhist monks telepathing on an IBM advertisement; movies like "Meet Joe Black," "Phenomenon," and "What Dreams May Come;" TV series such as "The X-Files," "Touched by An Angel," and "Millennium," or values-based leadership—the open expression of spirituality has become an ingrained part of our personal and professional lives. Its necessity for workplace adaptation will only intensify in the 21st Century.

Spirituality Is Inevitable

If spirituality is, in fact, inevitable, how do we engage the process? The answer is through personal and collective transformation. *Transformation is the process of letting go of beliefs that no longer serve a constructive purpose.* An example of personal transformation is the realization that an individual's personal success should never be at the expense of a team's success. This realization is a radical shift for an individual who has valued, practiced, and been rewarded for rugged individualism most of his or her life. An example of collective transformation would be an organizational shift in operation from entitlement to empowerment, as described in the following scenario.

When Texas Instruments began an extensive team-based operation in the late 1980s, a strong emphasis was placed on empowerment. Employees were expected to learn the meaning of empowerment and how to implement it. Some employees struggled with the transition from the previous operation of management-based motivation to self-motivation; from directed work assignments to delegation based upon proven performance; and ultimately, from employment as a right to employment as a privilege.

One business unit was required to make this shift over a few years in order to achieve its projected cost savings. The transition required employees to confront and invalidate beliefs that were self-limiting about their performance capabilities. These beliefs included, "We do what we are told," "We don't have the authority to responsibly act on our own," and "I might not be able to live up to the expectations of empowerment."

In order to accomplish their objectives, teams were established and delegated a series of stretch goals. Stretch goals, by definition, require new learning. They also challenge the validity of self-limiting beliefs, such as those cited above. As the various teams began to successfully achieve their goals they became more confident in their ability to perform in a self-directed manner. They began to learn that in reality there are few, if any, limitations to their capabilities. The question was their *willingness* to confront those apparent limitations. Confronting and invalidating self-imposed limitations, by the process of achieving challenging goals, is the essence of transformation. Therefore, transformation, driven by higher performance standards, is an inevitable *and* continuing part of work life.

The Rebirth of Joel Watson

Transformation is the primary way we adapt to change. Sometimes transformation is forced upon us as illustrated by the story of Joel Watson.

Joel Watson is the President and CEO of a small business that manufactures containers for commercial food products. As his business grew, he paid particular attention to the ratio of his company's income to the number of people he employed. Joel wanted this ratio to be as great as possible. This basic operational principle meant that he was often forced to work overtime hours on a regular basis. Joel did much of the quality assurance himself in order to ensure the service expected of his prestigious customers. He constantly pushed others to live up to his standard of zero-defect management in their work. He was only partially successful in this quest and often found himself checking their work to make sure quality was achieved.

One evening, while working late, Joel suffered a heart attack and almost died. During his recovery period in the hospital he had time to seriously reflect on how he lived his life and what was important to him. He realized his work was not fun anymore compared to when he started the company. He also realized that he believed he was an indispensable part of the entire operation. Without his constant attention to detail, something would "fall through the cracks." This belief was not only invalidated, but shattered during his convalescence.

When he returned to work, Joel was much more tolerant of the struggles his employees had to go through in order to achieve the same quality standard he had. He concluded that if the company was to survive and prosper, he *and* his employees would have to make it happen together, driven by shared leadership. As a result of this new approach, Joel felt "reconnected" to the natural enthusiasm he had when he started the business. His employees responded enthusiastically when it became clear that the success or failure of the company was going to depend on their commitment, alignment, and leadership. The business experienced a rebirth, probably because Joel underwent a rebirth.

By his own accounting, Joel experienced a traumatic form of transformation—an "existential crisis." This means a crisis of being. This type of transformation redefines "who we are," which is the driving force behind our participation in life. Ultimately, this driving force is sourced from our inner self. Joel's story graphically illustrates how personal crisis can often be the impetus for spiritual awakening.

Leading the Spiritual Charge!

Many CEOs and high-level executives, though somewhat limited by the constraints of their business environments, have been operating from a spiritual perspective in their own unique ways. For example, a CEO like the late Jerry Junkins of Texas Instruments espoused, instituted, and practiced humanistic principles. He operated compatibly within the business necessities of his organization, secure in the knowledge that his interactions with others were spiritually sourced. Les Alberthal, former President and CEO of Electronic Data Systems (EDS), is another individual whose leadership style reflected a deep concern for people. Additional examples include Jim Blanchard, Chairman and CEO of Synovous Financial in Columbus, Georgia, and Herb Kellerman, President and CEO of Southwest Airlines. The type of leadership established by these individuals has the ingrained characteristics of ethical values and humanistic principles. I suspect that well over 50% of the workforce today integrates spirituality into their lives in ways that are personally appropriate. Examples include a practical balance of work and home life; a spiritually sourced goal of success; care of the body through integration with the spirit; commitment to preserving the environment; reconnecting with Native American values; and practicing diets without meat or animal-based products.

When an individual faces his or her own mortality, such as Joel Watson did in the previous section, he or she commonly becomes fearless in promoting the resulting revelation. For example, a spiritually sourced value system that Joel convinced his organization to embrace, is the following:

1) Treat others with dignity, respect, and love.

2) View human equality as a basis for ethical behavior.

3) Realize that everything that exists is interdependent and interconnected—nature, animals, and humans.

4) View our organization, community, country, and world as one.

Joel's organization experienced a profound shift in operation when this value system became a reality. They also experienced a significant increase in performance, profitability, and employee growth and well-being.

As the time between cause and effect becomes progressively shorter, organizations require a value system based upon *preventing* crises. This means the incorporation of values that preserves the dignity, health, and well-being of *all* employees, and by logical extension, values that reflect responsibility for society and the environment. For example, when the first Europeans colonized the Americas, they inhabited a pristine land that had been occupied by the natives of this continent for approximately twenty-five centuries. Compare that with the impact, in the name of progress, that we have had on the same environment in less than four hundred years.

The basis of the new value system, referred to above, must be spiritual in conception and practice in order to be far-reaching and effective on a long-term basis. We must view ourselves as inherently related to nature, animals, and each other. This relationship plays out by realizing that whatever we produce that adversely affects the planetary environment will ultimately affect us and in progressively shorter time frames. This way of thinking is presently inspiring spiritual practices into the work environment, if not by designated leaders, then by the unpublicized actions of workers.

Spirituality Means Moral Responsibility

Do we have a moral responsibility for each other? If so, what is the source of such a motivation? What is the driving force that "naturally inspires" us to assume responsibility and take action to create change where inequality exists? The driving force is our spirituality and it is commonly activated by an event that changes our life. An example of such a life-changing event, in a case involving human equality, is the story of Les Harrison.

Les was foreman of a processing plant for a southern California corporation. The corporation employed a large number of Mexican-Americans. Many of the Mexican-American employees spoke English as a second language. Les was a native of the southern U.S. and had grown up in a homogenous neighborhood. Generally, outsiders were at best suspect and, at worst, unwelcomed. Les did not understand Spanish and felt uneasy when employees spoke Spanish while working. As a result, only Mexican-Americans who spoke virtually flawless English were promoted to management positions at the plant. Even though this practice was questioned, Les's superiors took a "hands-off" role in his operation of the plant as long as he met his production quotas.

One evening while overseeing the late night shift, Les's arm became caught in one of the machines. He immediately went into shock as a result of a broken arm and extensive tissue and muscle damage. His breathing became labored and irregular and he was bleeding as a result of the broken bone that penetrated his skin. Luis, a Mexican-American employee who had worked as a paramedic, immediately began mouth-to-mouth resuscitation. After Les began breathing regularly, Luis applied a tourniquet to Les's upper arm to stop the bleeding. He then set the broken arm and applied a makeshift ice pack to keep the swelling down. Luis also found blankets from the safety locker to keep Les warm to avoid the effects of shock. Shortly afterward, the paramedics arrived and took him to the hospital.

Les later learned that the expert care rendered by Luis prevented him from having a permanently damaged arm. As he lay recovering in the hospital, Les reflected on how he had treated Luis in the past. He had generally regarded him as aggressive and counterproductive because Luis often questioned Les's management style and record of promotions. On one occasion, Luis came close to accusing Les of regarding Mexican-Americans as inferior. Lying in his hospital bed, Les realized that underneath it all, this accusation was probably true. He realized that he resented the idea of Mexican-Americans making significant gains that came as a result of the years of protest by African-Americans. As these realizations flowed into his consciousness, Les simultaneously experienced overwhelming feelings of shame, guilt, and humility.

What I have not revealed to this point is that Les is an African-American. As he reflected upon his own upbringing in the South, he realized that he was doing exactly what had been done to him. He was just as prejudiced as anyone else, but until his current position, had rarely had the opportunity to inflict it upon others. Now, as a manager, he had established a practice of advancing those with whom he felt most comfortable. When he did not understand something, like the Spanish language, suspicion and fear controlled his behavior.

Somewhere deep inside, Les connected with a part of himself that vowed that he would never again consciously discriminate against anyone. He returned to work a different person and became fearless in promoting the diversity efforts of his organization. He set goals for representation on the policy committee to reflect his organization's ethnic composition. He let it be known that he would not tolerate any form of discrimination from anyone in his organization.

Les's realization led to a transformation in his beliefs about human equality. When he connected to his inner spirituality, he recognized his past behavior to be a *moral violation* of the code of ethics he had been taught. As a result, he accepted moral responsibility for the work environment he had created and became an active agent to change it.

It is vitally important to understand that where inequity exists, we are either active agents of change or supporters of the status quo. There is no neutral position! In addition to a moral responsibility for the workplace, we also have a social responsibility for the environment.

Spirituality and Social Responsibility

One of the major objectives of the "Gaia movement," based on the name given to Mother Earth, is for us to view the earth as a living organism. And to understand that we depend on the health of this living organism for our continued existence. My observation is that, as a culture, we generally view the earth as an inanimate object which we may use and abuse at our convenience. We often do for monetary profit based upon the erroneous assumption that technology will repair the damage we produce. In spite of the apparent short-term value we derive from economic business successes, we have not truthfully acknowledged the permanent toll the earth pays for our shortsighted activities.

For example, few of us are aware that gold mining is alive and well in the West. The U.S. has an 1872 law titled the "General Mining Law" that allows anyone from any country to buy U.S. property for gold mining at $5 an acre. The well-documented results of gold mining are polluted rivers, loss of animal life, scarred landscapes, and permanently reduced underground water tables. The gold-mining fever is fueled by *our* demand for gold jewelry. Therefore, we are *all* participants in this human-environmental drama and either we will all pay the consequences, or our children will.

In 1996, there were proposed gold-mining operations due to begin near Yellowstone National Park and the Black Hills of South Dakota. Although promises were made about environmental safeguards, accidents do occur spewing poisonous sulfuric acid into streams. Local populations were split between long-term environmental impact on one hand, and short-term jobs and economic boosts to local businesses on the other. In the end, the Yellowstone mining proposition was defeated in 1998.

The gold-mining project of Summitville, Colorado, is a good example of the unpredictability of mining operations that occur in environmentally fragile areas. Due to poor mine design and heavy snowfall, a break in the support structure resulted in a seventeen-mile stretch of a toxic and soot-polluted stream. The Canadian company who operated the mine declared bankruptcy, and the U.S. taxpayers were left to fund the cleanup. This phenomenon is referred to as the "gold shaft." The mining company gets the gold and the U.S. taxpayers get the shaft!

The state of Nevada supplies about one half of the gold mined in the U.S. through extensive open-pit mining. In a desert state where water is the lifeblood of its existence, mining operations not only pump tremendous quantities of water from underground streams but, as a result, lower the water table that ranchers and others depend upon for survival. The result of mining is the contamination of water with heavy metals such as arsenic, mercury, selenium, and chromium. Surface pools of poisonous lakes kill birds and deer regularly in spite of attempted safeguards. The mining operations simply pay the levied fines. So what is the point of these accounts? What can we do differently in a world of continual accelerated consumption? We can begin to take responsibility, as individuals, for our roles in propagating "runaway consumption." And then, take action to change our thinking and everyday behaviors, based upon our respective levels of commitment to preserving the planet for human existence.

We Are One with the Planet, Not Masters of It

The real issue comes down to values. Do we place more value on our so-called freedom to exploit the planet than we do on our responsibility for the environment? Do we require a crisis to create outrage and action? Unless we change our current mode of behavior, this dichotomy will only continue to lead to the demise of the planet; and correspondingly, an environment uninhabitable for our continued existence.

Fundamentally, we require a spiritual transformation to bring us to the realization that we are one with the planet and not masters who presume to conquer it. Fortunately, there is a growing movement in the U.S. and elsewhere where organizations and individuals are assuming greater environmental responsibility without the necessity for local or federal legislation. Organizations like the Sierra Club, Environmental Defense Fund, and other environmental groups are tireless in their efforts to keep the public informed and actively participating in environmental preservation.

In addition, there are a growing number of socially responsible companies that are reassessing the dangers of their products or by-products to the environment, animals, and ultimately humans, via the food chain. These reassessments are also done without the necessity of governmental intervention. Instead, they occur before, during, and after production as a matter of social responsibility. These organizations view environmental sensitivity and profitability as mutually compatible. They also view environmental responsibility as a social obligation. As a result, they take the lead in establishing a cooperative relationship with environmentally conscious groups wherein the welfare of the planetary ecosystem is of overriding importance. An adversarial relationship is unacceptable to both groups.

An organization that has voluntarily accepted social responsibility for the environment is Patagonia,[4] a designer and distributor of outdoor clothing. In reassessing their operation, the leadership of the company decided that all of Patagonia's facilities would be involved in recycling and composting, and would have edible landscaping, low-energy-use power, and insulation. They further decided to use recycled paper everywhere, encourage ride sharing, and eliminate their usage of paper cups. From a long-term perspective, they began to reassess the environmental impact of the clothing they manufacture. Actions have been taken at the company to address pollution, insecticides, and the volume of wool taken from flocks of sheep and goats that often denude environmentally fragile land.

The Earth Will Exist, With or Without Us

The *real* question we have to come to grips with is one of "wants versus needs." What do we sensibly need or require in the way of possessions and services that will still allow us to exist compatibly with the planetary environment and *all* of its inhabitants? In answering this question it is important to keep in mind that most of us have not yet really accepted the fact that the planet Earth is finite. It has finite resources and genuine vulnerabilities in regard to maintaining its balance. Yet we continue to build, dam, produce, and consume at an accelerated pace with little or no regard for the short-term or long-term environmental implications.

The solution to this dilemma is the adoption of a "new consciousness" with respect to the Earth system. It is the realization that humankind is an integral part of the interconnected Earth system; and that every element, phenomenon, or species is alive with spirit. *We have no dominion over the Earth system!* We are simply a part of it. Therefore, we have no power to save or destroy it. We merely have the ability to influence the existence and transformation of a number of Earth's life-forms. It is essential for us to realize this fact. For when the Earth system experiences a sufficiently high degree of imbalance (because of humankind's abuse), it will cleanse itself of the unnatural deposits and stresses created by our pollution, building, damming, and destroying. Therefore, preserving the planet is *really* sustaining our own existence. The planet will prevail with or without us!

Spirituality and Cooperation

There is a growing realization that long-term business success is based more upon cooperation than pitted competition. The nature of this realization is spiritual. It is an acknowledgment of the inherent connectedness that exists among similar types of businesses. The obvious forms that this realization takes are strategic alliances, partnerships, and even referrals for, and support of, other businesses' successes. An underlying trust implied by this practice is that the marketplace is always sufficiently abundant for organizations that are willing to promote their own success as well as the success of others. This realization of interdependence is another of the characteristics practiced by Living Organizations. This shift in thinking, from scarcity to abundance, is also spiritual in nature. Examples of cooperative business relationships are Microsoft and Intel, Apple Computer and Motorola, Innovations International and In Partnership Consulting of Oakland, California, and the Health Alliance of Greater Cincinnati, Ohio.

Intel provides the chips that power the Microsoft software programs on personal computers. Motorola produces the central process unit (CPU) that powers the

Apple Computer. Innovations and In Partnership Consulting would normally be seen as competitors, but have actually formed a strategic alliance to promote non-redundant programs, seminars, and consulting expertise offered by the two corporations. They work together as a "seamless partnership" while simultaneously maintaining their separate business operations. Innovations brings its expertise in seminar design and facilitation, and marketing and sales. In Partnership Consulting brings exceptional expertise in seminar presentation, facilitation, and consulting. In order to more efficiently provide medical services for the Greater Cincinnati area, the Health Alliance brought together The Christ Hospital, University Hospital, The St. Luke Hospitals, and The Jewish Hospitals. This alliance specializes in cardiac care, women's healthcare, healthcare for older adults, trauma care, and advanced cancer treatment facilities. It provides a tri-state area with coordinated diagnostic and treatment support of leading specialists, hospitals, and research facilities.

Globalization and Diversity Are Synonymous

The point to realize from these examples of inter-company cooperation is that we are a global, interlinked business economy, rather than competing segments, such as the Pacific Rim, the North American Free Trade Association (NAFTA), and the European Economic Community. In fact, these regions are crucial parts of the interdependent global system. The Asian business crisis of 1998 measurably affected every region of the world, both large and small. Business transactions cut across ideological boundaries unlike any other societal system.

Such transactions provide the opportunity for us to forge new paradigms of thinking that create a common context of operation across continents.

For example, as corporations based in specific countries begin to seriously globalize, they will be faced with the need to operate with a common set of core values, principles, and systems of ethics that are designed to accommodate the culture of each particular country. The objective is to allow for work practices that are in concert with a given culture's fundamental value system, as long as the necessary business performance measures are achieved (i.e., the operation is profitable, productive, and employee-supportive).

In the Eastern part of the world, the value of group is so strongly embedded that teamwork would be a dominant part of that region's work practices. In the Western world, there will probably always be a strong emphasis on individual contribution. The real challenge of globalization will be to create a "new business paradigm" that compatibly embraces both, as well as the variety of diametrically different global cultural values. This is what is meant by "global compatibility from a business perspective." In this sense, globalization and diversity are synonymous.

Ten exercises to help you reconnect to your spirituality are suggested on the following pages.

TEN EXERCISES TO RECONNECT WITH YOUR SPIRITUALITY

1. Meditate daily for ten to fifteen minutes.

    First, practice sitting (or lying) quietly and *thinking* about whatever thoughts cross your mind.

    Then, practice sitting (or lying) quietly and *listening* to your thoughts. When your mind stops listening, you will be connected to your spirituality.

2. Cross-country ski or hike off the beaten path and consciously focus on your surroundings without thinking or judging. Just attempt to be part of the environment, like the snow, a tree, or a rabbit.

3. Hold a baby, look into its eyes, and let your mind spontaneously intuit the message the child is sending to you.

4. Do a visualization exercise where you create a trusted advisor. Ask that advisor, "What is my greatest barrier to connecting with my spirituality?" Listen quietly for the spontaneous answer you get. This exercise may take several tries.

5. Before going to sleep, ask your subconscious mind to take you on a journey to explore your spiritual consciousness as a dream. This request must be serious for your subconscious to take you seriously!

6. Walk on a beach, preferably at night, and notice what a minute, but significant part you are of a very big picture. Write about your experience.

7. Watch a morning sunrise as though seeing it for the first time. Avoid judging; just *be* with it.

8. Next time you are in the "zone," write in detail the events and context that prepared you for this experience. Practice preparing yourself to experience the "zone" whenever you choose.

9. When you feel sorry for yourself, visit with someone worse off than you and try to experience *empathy, compassion, humility* and *love.* These are all spiritually sourced experiences.

10. Actively engage in activities to develop your intuitive side: personal development books, tapes, trainings, and materials dealing with the subject of spirituality.

Celebrate your successes! You are home!

Chapter Three

People—The Only Sustainable Competitive Advantage

"It is wonderful when people of divergent views come together, not to emphasize their differences, but their points of unity."

Paramahansa Yogananda

Introduction

The key to an organization's continuing success is attracting and retaining knowledgeable and continually learning individuals. A knowledgeable individual is one who has developed the ability to creatively integrate information. Thus,

$$\textbf{Information} \xrightarrow[\text{integrated}]{\text{creatively}} \textbf{Knowledge}$$

Knowledge that is used in experiential learning, such as working through a difficulty, a challenge, or a crisis, results in wisdom. The continuous cycle of acquiring greater wisdom is:

$$\textbf{Knowledge} \xrightarrow[\text{learning}]{\text{experiential}} \textbf{Wisdom}$$

Ultimately, wisdom is a way of being that is reflected by an individual's in-depth understanding of self and others. This level of understanding is an emerging skill necessary for leadership and management in today's work force. The source of wisdom is one's spirituality. Spirituality is also the source of imagination, creativity, intuition, vision, insight, inspiration, and quantum-thinking. The extent to which these characteristics are an ingrained part of an organization's culture will, in large part, determine its future success.

These characteristics are inherent in people, not in machines, software programs, or even in artificial intelligence. They are spiritual in nature because they involve mental processes that go beyond ordinary or rational thinking. These characteristics correspond to the essential abilities that must be developed by employees in order to achieve high performance. Therefore, empowered, high-performing people are an organization's only sustainable competitive advantage.

In this chapter we will learn how to become empowered, high-performing individuals. We will also learn that high performance is not possible without a committed leadership support system.

The Foundation of High Performance

The foundation upon which high performance is based is a high degree of personal responsibility and personal accountability. *Personal responsibility is the willingness to view one's self as the principal source of the results and circumstances which occur in one's life; both individually and collectively with others.* The more we view ourselves as the principal source, the more we are able to proactively respond to difficulties or challenges in our lives.

Without this sense of personal ownership, it is virtually impossible to begin to tap the potential of our creative ability. In-depth creativity requires an intention to accept total responsibility for establishing the conditions for breakthrough ideas to occur.

Personal accountability is the willingness to own the results which occur in one's life; both individually and collectively with others. The key phrase in this definition is "own the results." Accepting ownership, even when it is unfair or unreasonable, empowers us to proactively transform "win-lose" situations into successful "win-win" scenarios. These two concepts are illustrated by the business challenge of Stan Anderson.

Stan Anderson—A Tale of Woe and Wisdom

Stan Anderson entered into a contractual agreement to produce a new breakthrough product in multimedia software. He had the technical knowledge and his contractual partner was an expert in software design. They agreed to share the profits from the sale of the software product equally during the first year. Both agreed they would make a "best effort" at selling the product separately and together. Soon thereafter, Stan's partner experienced cash flow problems and had to re-prioritize his business objectives. As a result, he did very little in promoting the product. Stan, however, borrowed heavily to promote and sell the software product.

During the first six months, sales were poor. Stan became angry at his partner and considered suing him for breach of contract. He felt he had been betrayed. As he went though this process, he noticed that some of his friends felt sorry for him, but a few kept asking him what would he do if he had no partner. They reminded him that the business environment is unpredictable and that success is based upon how you respond to adversity. At his lowest point in this process, Stan decided it was more important to be successful than it was to be a victim. His attitude about responsibility began to change. He had always felt himself to be highly responsible, but it had never been tested to this extent before. Sure, what happened to him was unfair, but did that excuse him from being responsible for doing everything *he* could to make his software product successful? Stan decided that he was ultimately responsible despite the circumstances. He decided to fully commit to making the software product a success regardless of what his partner did to promote the product.

It is amazing how events happen in our favor once we decide to become committed to the end regardless of the final result. A week later, Stan was contacted by a national video marketing and distributing company that was interested in representing his software product. His product had been highly recommended by someone who had previewed it and thought that it was great! The German poet Goethe wrote a passage which states that once an individual totally commits to something, all forms of support begin to appear that he or she could have never known or predicted. He describes this phenomenon as a mystery of the human spirit. What appeared for Stan was exactly what he needed in proportions much greater than he had ever expected.

What we learn from this example is that responsibility and accountability go beyond ethics, values, and even signed agreements. Even when these expectations are violated by others, we are still responsible and accountable for the outcome. Situations like Stan experienced often *force* us to look inside ourselves, to depths never explored before, for courage and faith. These qualities are spiritual in nature because they go beyond rationality and proof. When we begin to view ourselves as 100% responsible and 100% accountable for the events in our lives, responsibility and accountability become spiritual concepts. We cease to ask, "Why did this happen to me?" since most explanations are totally unreasonable. Unreasonable explanations go beyond the mind for ultimate resolution within our spiritual consciousness.

This example illustrates a three-step process for acquiring wisdom that you might practice in your everyday life:

1) *The acceptance of reality*—the willingness to move beyond denial, anger, bargaining, and guilt, and accept a situation as it is.[5]

2) *The experience of humility*—the complete reduction of the ego's agenda for revenge when you experience unfairness.

3) *The achievement of inner peace*—the adoption of a neutral, nonjudgmental attitude towards events and others in your life.

We now have in place the foundation for becoming a high-performing individual: the acceptance of 100% personal responsibility and accountability for our lives. We can now build upon this foundation with unique personal competencies. When these competencies are put into practice to produce outstanding performance, we can begin to understand the true meaning of the word empowerment.

An Empowered Individual

Empowerment is one of the most important concepts for success in the 21st Century, and yet one of the most confusing. *Empowerment is not the act of delegation!* Delegation is essential for implementation, but it is not the definition of empowerment. *Empowerment is the capacity to perform.* With respect to the workplace, it is the *ability to produce* something of sufficient value that an employer or a customer is willing to pay for it. Empowerment does not mean irresponsibly delegating to someone in a manner that is disproportionate to their ability. It does mean, however, that one needs to establish a measurable means of accountability *before* the fact. Most of all, empowerment is not something we can *give* each other. "To be empowered" is to have the ability and to be granted the authority to carry out one's responsibilities within guidelines that have been mutually agreed upon, in advance, by both the supervisor and the individual. The freedom to carry out one's responsibilities with the least amount of oversight or management is *earned* on the basis of competency and proven performance.

Therefore, an empowered individual is one who is:

1) Highly competent

2) Self-managed

3) Continuously learning

Self-management is the most difficult requirement for both employees and managers to master. It involves the ability to *plan, prioritize, focus,* and *execute* one's work responsibilities with the least amount of oversight or direction. It is vital to understand that *management* does not disappear when implementing empowerment—even though *managers* are de-emphasized. Instead, management is passed on to the individual or team who, as a result, assumes greater authority. Some practical ways the four characteristics mentioned here play out are the following.

For empowerment to work, management and oversight of employees' work must be minimized. This means that each employee must take personal responsibility for ensuring the quality of his or her work. Where products are fabricated, there should be minimal need for a quality assurance manager. Where computer systems are installed for a client, they work, period! Where repetitive documentation is a way of life, exceptional proficiency in grammar, spelling, and understanding the use of the documentation should be mastered. These are examples of self-management. This way of operating is based upon a high degree of personal responsibility and accountability.

Gwen Mallory—When the Going Gets Tough, the Tough Get Empowered

If the essence of empowerment is performance, then personal empowerment is the ability of an individual to perform. This ability is measured by one's mind-set, education, skills, and competencies. One of the greatest limitations we place on ourselves, in terms of mind-set, is the adoption of an aggressive attitude about success at the expense of quality interpersonal relationships. Such an attitude may have served as a motivation when we were younger, but may be counterproductive as an adult in the workplace. The result is limited performance irrespective of how competent we might be. This situation is illustrated by the experience of Gwen Mallory.

After graduating from a prestigious engineering school, Gwen Mallory accepted a position with a major utility company. Although she graduated in the top 5% of her class, her overall performance during the first year was rated as merely "good." Her colleagues described her as "pushy" and "overbearing." Soon they began avoiding Gwen. Her suggestions in team meetings were listened to, but rarely implemented. She began to resent the way she was treated. Her situation came to a head when a male engineer who had joined the company the same time she did was promoted ahead of her. Gwen promptly submitted her resignation and was hired by another company within two months.

Gwen vowed to make her new job successful and avoid the situation she experienced at the utility company. After all, the criticism might, in part, be true. She was determined not to get the reputation of being "pushy" or "overbearing" at her new job. But no matter how hard she tried to behave in opposition to these descriptions, her new colleagues began to experience her in this same way. Fortunately, a senior female engineer, Marsha Wheeling, invited Gwen to dinner to share her experience of what she had encountered and the critical realizations she had experienced in the process.

The first realization she shared with Gwen was that she had learned to accept, for the short-term, the *fact* that the playing field for women was not even. That situation would change gradually as more women assumed influential positions in the organization. Marsha went on to explain, however, that accepting that reality did not mean giving in to it, but rather it meant that one could begin to behave non-reactively to it when she encountered it. Gwen explained that she had competed with males most of her life, starting with wanting to be an engineer. She explained that she had developed a "toughness," mostly to protect herself from becoming discouraged and giving up. Marsha shared that she had also gone through a similar phase, but discovered that although that attitude served her well in high school and college, it was counterproductive to her career as an adult. In fact, such an attitude could actually sabotage her career. Finally, she explained to Gwen that there are two major beliefs prevalent in the workplace that women are forced to deal with: "women are too emotional to respond professionally in tough situations" and "women are not as committed in the long run to their careers." "Both of which can provoke behaviors that might be perceived as pushy or overbearing, as compensating mechanisms," Marsha explained.

"The only reason we respond counterproductively to these beliefs is because somewhere deep within *us*, we feel a guilt that there might be some truth to these," Marsha revealed. "The fact that they might also be true of men does not solve the problem for us."

"What should I do?" Gwen asked.

"First of all, just honestly think about what I have shared with you for the next week or two," Marsha replied. "See if deep within yourself these may also be your beliefs that you have been conditioned with since childhood. The toughness you developed was a coping mechanism to avoid becoming discouraged and giving up. Maybe you will discover that being tough doesn't serve you anymore. Then let's talk again."

Several weeks later, when Gwen and Marsha met again, Gwen shared how much she had discovered about herself by just thinking about those two beliefs. She realized that her reaction to people's comments and behaviors triggered something inside of her. She felt she was prepared to learn more about handling situations where her "toughness" was perceived by others as "pushy." Marsha suggested she focus inwardly on her feelings and emotions when she encountered a triggering comment or behavior. She advised Gwen to take a couple of undetected deep breaths. And then decide how to best respond to the issue at hand as though the point raised was valid. Using Marsha's suggestions, Gwen noticed a difference in the way her colleagues began to respond to her ideas. They also began to include her in their social activities. Over a period of several months, her reputation as "pushy" and "overbearing" began to disappear.

What we learn from this example are three insights. First, Gwen was more committed to being successful than allowing a self-defeating attitude to restrict her performance. Second, by non-reactively accepting the reality of undesirable workplace beliefs and attitudes, she freed herself to respond in a constructive and proactive manner. And third, having an experienced mentor like Marsha was key to Gwen's breakthrough in personal growth. Thus, we might conclude that the process of becoming more empowered is often facilitated by someone with greater wisdom about situations that we find too difficult to resolve ourselves.

A Model of an Empowered Individual

In the preceding discussions, we established that an empowered individual is one who performs consistent with the authority that is delegated. We also established that mind-set and competency were key elements in determining one's level of performance. Mind-set is determined by personality characteristics such as dedication, persistence, commitment, self-motivation, and self-responsibility. Natural and learned competencies include education, skills, talents, abilities, and strengths. Therefore, we conclude that mind-set drives competencies to achieve one's level of performance according to the following model:

An Empowered Individual

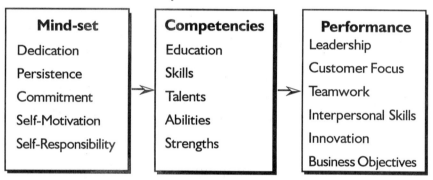

Figure 2. An empowered individual is driven to succeed by a desire to fully utilize his or her competencies.

Without a strong internal desire to succeed, an individual's level of performance can be marginal, even when he or she possesses outstanding competencies. Using this principle, we can clearly see that Gwen's difficulty was in the mind-set category—specifically, dealing with taking self-responsibility for the attitude that "toughness is necessary for a woman to be successful."

Becoming an Integrated Person

The dramatic changes occurring in the workplace today challenge most our mind-sets about expectations of performance as a condition for employment. The most fundamental expectation is the shift from entitlement to empowerment. U.S. corporations have historically operated in a patriarchal manner structured in a hierarchical system. This combination of structure and operation led most employees to believe they would be "taken care of for life" in exchange for company loyalty. We came to believe we were *entitled* to jobs and security for life. This unspoken agreement was fairly successful, according to business profit and loss measures, as long as the U.S. dominated the world economy. However, as the world's resources became more widely dispersed in the 1980s and 1990s, we found that we could no longer afford to maintain an entitlement system. Much of the work that required large numbers of people could be performed by fewer people using information systems. Thus, the historical pact between loyal employees and their companies was broken.

In a relatively short period of five to ten years, U.S. workers have been expected to suddenly shift to a mind-set of self-sufficiency—sometimes viewed by many as self-survival. We were expected to adopt and practice the mind-set shown on page 69, in Figure 2 of "An Empowered Individual." In other words, the leadership of most U.S. corporations decided to break the historical parent-child relationship. Our response to this shift in operation was fairly predictable. "We don't like it! We don't accept it! And furthermore, we will do everything possible to sabotage its implementation!" This is very much like the reaction of a child being forced into adulthood.

The harsh realities of empowerment, quality, reengineering, diversity, and most of all downsizing, have forced us to grudgingly accept the new pact. These imperatives have also forced us to finally acknowledge that we have always been adults, even if we have been unwilling to assume that role in the past. In reality, this acknowledgment is the result of reconnecting to our inner source for personal resolution. Once reconnected to this source, it becomes a permanent part of the way we live our lives. We begin to *experience* what it means to be whole as a human being. We also realize that an empowered individual is one whose mind-set for success is driven from this source, beyond external rewards or acknowledgments. Reconnecting to this spiritual source is the key to becoming an integrated person.

The Integrated Person

An integrated person is one who has integrated body, mind, and spirit in the way he or she functions in everyday life. Integration is the result of the continual acquisition of wisdom through experiential learning. This type of individual is represented by the model shown in Figure 3 on the following page.

Although we use models to describe various aspects of ourselves, in reality, body, mind, and spirit are one integrated whole. The physical body has a consciousness that is an integration of our propensity for survival and our cultural heritage accumulated over generations. The mind is our personal consciousness, which is the way we have individually programmed our total accumulated

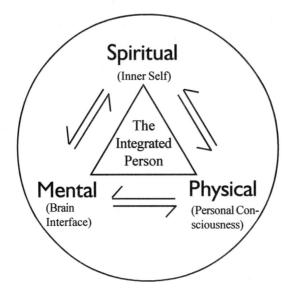

Figure 3. The integrated person is one who has integrated body, mind, and spirit.

knowledge. This is the ego. It is unique for each individual. The spiritual dimension is our creative consciousness. It is the source of wisdom. The brain serves as the interface for both physical–mental interaction and physical–spiritual interaction. Therefore, feelings and emotions are either mentally or spiritually sourced. For example, emotional conflict experienced as anger by the body is feedback suggesting that the way our minds are interpreting events we experience should be reexamined. Reacting counterproductively to life situations, rather than responding proactively, is sourced from survival-based beliefs that are most often invalid. These beliefs are programmed in our personal consciousness. Whereas, feelings of joy and exhilaration are spiritually sourced. The integrated person is able to distinguish life events that involve true survival from imagined survival.

The O. J. Simpson case was an excellent opportunity for each of us to learn about our personal programming in the areas of race and ethnicity.

The O. J. Case—A Mirror Reflection of the U.S.

Most of us experience racial differences irrationally. Perceived from our own reality, we are right, irrespective of the emotional conflict we might experience. This was clearly demonstrated by the O. J. Simpson trials and verdicts. The U.S. public reaction was a clear demonstration of our collective irrationality. Public opinion polls showed that our agreement or disagreement about the verdicts were divided along racial lines. Most blacks believed Simpson innocent and most whites believed him guilty. However, few of those polled had seen much of the trial and none had been jurors. What then was the basis for our decisions? It was our personal opinions, predetermined by our racial programming. Few of us would admit that at the core of our belief system, we are racially biased. Unless we have had to face that issue in some traumatic way, then, at best, our core beliefs about racial distinctions have never been tested. Therefore, what we learn from the O. J. Simpson incident is how "mentally and spiritually divided" we are as a nation of people, and probably, as a world.

Awareness begins by acknowledging that our reactions probably had little to do with the trials, but with our fundamental perceptions and beliefs about each other as a people. Diversity is the movement that attempts to challenge us to examine this most fundamental issue of human nature: *the presumed superiority or inferiority of a person based upon race or ethnicity.* However, as with most issues of this nature, the resolution will most likely be precipitated by crisis rather than addressed proactively. Unless a critical mass of us are willing to tell the truth, *as a prelude to action*, then crisis is inevitable.

The integrated person challenges himself or herself, without the necessity for external crisis, whenever he or she experiences emotional or mental conflict. The most direct indicators that harmony and balance are not present are reactions such as distress and illness. These are dramatic feedback mechanisms informing us that the way we are interpreting and responding to external events may be invalid. The message is to look inwardly for resolution. When ignored, we commonly experience even more severe physical ailments that, in some cases, may ultimately lead to premature death. When we choose to ignore personal growth, our bodies pay the price anyway!

The Spiritual Connection

When athletes experience the "zone," it is because mental processing shuts down and the physical body is driven directly from one's spiritual inner self. Time disappears. Events slow down. Outcomes are assured in concert with one's true intentionality. When meditating, mental processing stops and the spiritual self allows one the opportunity to spontaneously experience instances of insight, inspiration, and holistic seeing. Such experiences transform one's personal consciousness. This process is commonly referred to as spiritual growth because the result is greater integration of body, mind, and spirit. These experiences are also described as a state of "bliss."

Abraham Maslow, the father of humanistic psychology, has described the integrated (or self-actualized) person in the following way.[6]

"The integrated person is one who lives life naturally; is less split; more open to experience; less fearful; more spontaneous and expressive; ego transcended; closer to the core of being; more natural; one who trusts his or her own intuition, emotions, and thoughts; more accepting; and a 'fully-functional person.'"

The breakthrough realization to becoming integrated is the understanding that *we are spiritual beings having a physical experience rather than physical beings having a spiritual experience.* Individuals who become more integrated by acknowledging and embracing their spirituality open themselves to extraordinary performance. In order for extraordinary performance to become reality, there must be a leadership support system that complements and enhances the potential of a highly competent individual.

Models of Leadership

Having highly competent employees is only half the requirement for a high-performing organization. There must also be a system of operation that facilitates and supports the growth, learning, and well-being of those employees. Elements that most effectively support this process are a relatively flat organizational structure (minimal hierarchy), extensive information sharing, and the delegation of authority in proportion to an individual's competency. The two models of leadership that dominate organizational operation today are illustrated below by Figure 4, as extreme ends of a spectrum. They are hierarchy and self-management.

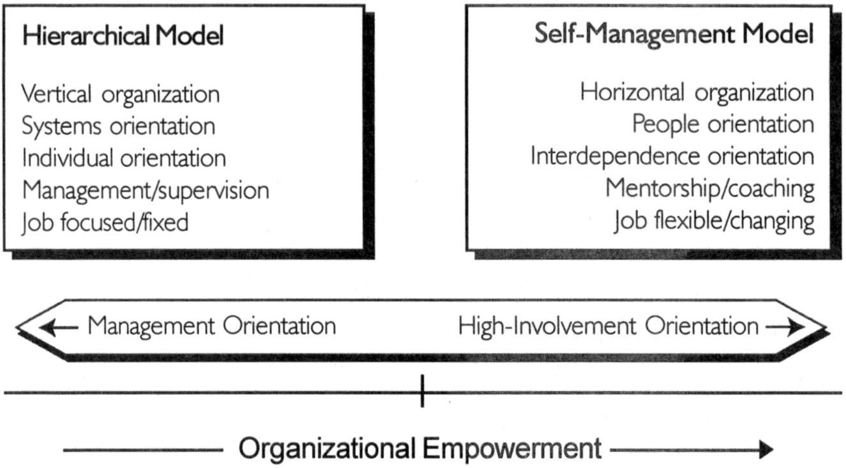

Hierarchical Model	Self-Management Model
Vertical organization	Horizontal organization
Systems orientation	People orientation
Individual orientation	Interdependence orientation
Management/supervision	Mentorship/coaching
Job focused/fixed	Job flexible/changing

← Management Orientation   High-Involvement Orientation →

———————— Organizational Empowerment ————→

Figure 4. Models of leadership spanning the spectrum from hierarchy to self-management.

Most organizations are moving from hierarchical operation toward greater self-management. This movement is driven by increasing customer demand for *quality, customization, speed,* and *service*.[7] Hierarchical-oriented systems are simply too cumbersome, slow, and outdated to adequately respond to these four performance requirements. Moving from left to right along Figure 4 means that the capability per employee increases in terms of competence, self-management, and continuous learning. Thus, as an average sum of all employees, the organization becomes more empowered.

It should be stressed that the necessity for movement from left to right is driven by the stringent demands of the marketplace. In practice, organizations operate most effectively by using a combination of management orientation *and* high-involvement orientation. The appropriate combination of these orientations is governed by meeting the requirements of an empowered organization discussed on page 16—profitable, productive, and employee-supportive.

Spiritual Leadership

The force that drives an organization to proactively become more empowered is *spiritual leadership*. Spiritual leadership is the establishment of an environment where humanistic values are integrated with sound business practices to govern the way an organization achieves its business objectives. Spiritually driven leaders inspire employees by *living* the values and *modelling* the principles espoused by their organization. When an organization becomes a highly empowered operation, it simultaneously becomes high performing. At this point, organizational confidence replaces competitive survival as an organizational motivation. The motivation to be a Living Organization is creative adaptation in response to accelerated change. Change, although still unnerving, is more easily accepted as an inherent part of the human condition and not something to be feared. It is viewed more as a constant source of environmental feedback requiring our natural creative ability for adaptation. Change opens us to our full capacity to be creative and innovative.

W. L. Gore—The Ultimate in Self-Management

The classic example of an organization that has operated in a self-managed way since its inception in the 1950s is W. L. Gore and Associates. They are probably best known for the breathable, waterproof material called Gore-Tex. The organization was established by Bill Gore Sr. and his family after he decided to leave the Dupont company. Bill was intensely interested in an organization of people who, in a very large part, were self-organizing. That is, left to their own devices, employees could find solutions to difficulties they experience by tapping into their inherent creative abilities. In essence, he assumed that human beings have an innate ability to organize themselves in such a manner as to achieve any objective to which they are committed. This assumption might be described as a leap of faith in the human spirit since at W. L. Gore and Associates, no formal provision is made for leadership in the traditional sense. In addition, the word "management" is banned from the vocabulary of the organization.

To an outsider, their mode of operation might appear to be loose and sometimes chaotic. An associate who heads the Flagstaff, Arizona, division is John Giovale. He is strongly influenced by Gore's principles and is a tireless disciple for ensuring that their value system is never compromised in the interest of short-term profit. John has been a spiritually driven leader for the entire fifteen years that I have known him. He refuses to be singled out for acknowledgment, insists on getting maximum input on the discussion of all important issues, and encourages younger associates to begin learning how to solve (or resolve) their own problems. Structurally, the organization is a two-dimensional matrix. This means anyone can go to anyone from whom they require something to successfully complete their projects. Work is structured around projects, almost totally involving teams.

When someone joins the company, instead of being told what to do, the person is encouraged to "wander around" talking to project groups until he or she finds something interesting to work on. The organization abhors paper and rules. Once I facilitated a seminar where we generated some wonderful ideas for conducting a new project. After the seminar, they promptly asked me to either destroy the materials written on flipcharts or take them back to Salt Lake City with me.

The Way of the Future

In a previous section, I stated that spiritual leadership is a context of operation where humanistic values are integrated with sound business practices. There is no more fundamental spiritual value than an inherent belief (or trust) in the capacity of people to constructively resolve any human conflict or challenge—and to creatively innovate new products and services necessary for longevity. The unspoken and unwritten principles of operation that characterize the Gore organization are the following:

1. Our long-term existence as an organization is dependent on continually developing the competency of our people.

2. The organizational structure that best supports the continuing development of our people is one with little or no hierarchy.

3. The system of operation that best supports (1.) and (2.) above is one where our employees are extensively involved in policy making, decision making, and operations.

Two crucial requirements for organizations operating in this manner are highly responsible and self-managed employees. In fact, the average employee who successfully adapts to the Gore culture is not the average U.S. American worker. Thus, the total number of Gore employees worldwide is only about 7,000. Obviously, this mode of operation would not be appropriate for most organizations. However, the spiritual principles espoused by Gore are progressively becoming necessities for all organizations aspiring to exist into the 21st Century.

As a postscript to this storybook description, the patent for Gore-Tex expired in 1995. As a result, Gore found itself in the throes of new competition. During 1996, they were intensely involved in the process of recreating themselves, but not at the expense of those enduring values and principles that have kept them in a class alone. As of 1999, they have successfully navigated the transition to a more competitive environment. A key element is the formation of a strategic alliance with a high tech corporation with the stated purpose being to again set the industry standard—this time in terms of medical support products and devices.

Ten ways to become an empowered, high-performing, and integrated individual are described on the following pages.

Ten Ways of Becoming an Empowered, High-Performing, Integrated Individual

The following statements are a list of guidelines to assist you in becoming an integrated individual.

1. The only job security that exists is to have competencies that are of value to someone—so take responsibility for becoming highly competent, self-managed, and continuously learning.

2. Evaluate your competencies and their relevance to what is wanted and needed by someone. Then create a personalized professional development (career) plan.

3. Based upon the "new workplace rules" for employment, create your own personal minimum expectations necessary for you to be committed to an organization.

   Be personally responsible for your professional fate; no one else will.

4. Take workshops to experience your spirituality and integrate it into your day-to-day life.

5. Take a serious diversity training in order to experience whether you contribute to the spirit of your organization or drain it by supporting the status quo.

6. If your organization does not live, enforce, and apply spiritually sourced values such as respect, integrity, equality, and equal opportunity that are aligned with your personal values, then consider another organization. Otherwise, you may never realize your full potential.

7. Define for yourself what comprises meaningful work and use it to redefine your work responsibilities.

8. Take responsibility for learning how to be naturally creative and innovative in your work. If you don't, you will jeopardize your value to the organization.

9. Find a quiet place, go into deep relaxation, create a mirror image of yourself, and respond to the following questions with respect to your workplace performance:

   a) What is my greatest physical barrier?

   b) What is my greatest mental barrier?

   c) What is my greatest spiritual barrier?

   d) What do I plan to do to overcome each of these?

   Then, "Just Do It!" and don't make a big deal of it!

10. Find an organization that supports the professional development of *all* of its people and join it.

    Your success is in your hands. Partner with an organization that truly values and appreciates you!

Chapter Four

Service—An Unconditional Commitment to Others

*"One thing I know: the only ones among you
who will really be happy are those who will
have sought and found how to serve."*

Dr. Albert Schweitzer

Introduction

Service is an unconditional commitment to the success and well-being of others and is based upon the realization of our natural relatedness to each other. This bond of this interrelatedness is not only physical, but mental, emotional, and spiritual as well. When this sense of connectedness is realized, we *naturally* feel a responsibility to act in a way that is mutually beneficial to ourselves and others. Paradoxically, the action taken is driven from an impetus to support the success of someone else and yet, in doing so, we simultaneously serve and nurture ourselves. The two experiences of serving self and others are inseparable because, spiritually, we are inseparable. The natural drive to serve is the essence of servant-leadership, as espoused by Robert K. Greenleaf, that we referred to earlier in Chapter One.

This chapter will show how service, from a spiritual perspective, is related to the experience of humility. It will also show that continuous quality improvement, creativity and innovation, and quantum-thinking are organizational skills that are necessary for us to meet and exceed the expanding expectations of customers.

Service Requires Humility

When we think of serving, we generally think of people like Jesus Christ, Mahatma Gandhi, Martin Luther King Jr., Albert Schweitzer, and Mother Teresa. We hold these individuals in a special class because of the impact they have had in transforming the consciousness of the world. Transforming consciousness is, by definition, a spiritual pursuit. Each of these individuals operated from a context of selflessness and an ownership of the conditions of others. Selflessness is the result of the personal realization of humility. Humility simply means that one realizes his or her *equality* and *connectedness* to others. This state of being is usually achieved by encountering, transcending, and being transformed by some life situation, condition, or event.

Jesus is said to have gone into the desert for his transformation. Gandhi experienced what it was like to be East Indian in a white South African culture in the 1890s. King had the Civil Rights Movement literally thrust upon him as his experience of "fire and brimstone." Each of us experiences this same process in our own unique manner. We may not impact as many people or transform the consciousness of the planet, but each of our experiences of transformation is just as powerful as theirs. The magnitude of the impact is simply proportional to the sphere of responsibility we view ourselves as having. Therefore, each of the individuals cited above would probably not consider their transformation as being greater in importance than what each of us experiences. The major difference is the size of the board upon which we choose to play the game. The life-changing experience of Jack Olsen illustrates this process.

Jack Olsen—"I Need All the Money That Exists to Be Secure"

Jack Olsen is a medical doctor who would be described as very successful—successful in terms of the money he earned. For most of his life, Jack was driven by a desire to be rich. He had a private practice *and* he worked at a hospital clinic four hours in the evening. As a result, he had very little time for his wife and family. He always told them that his long working hours were necessary to provide a better life for them. Although they did not really believe this explanation, they did enjoy the "fruits of his labor" such as vacations, cars, and numerous consumer items. Everybody was getting what they *thought* they needed and wanted.

Then one night, after working a twelve-hour day at his practice, Jack had a life-changing experience while driving to the clinic. A lack of sleep and preoccupation with financial expenditures had dulled his concentration for just a split second. In that instant, a semi-truck almost collided head-on with Jack's Mercedes. Afterwards, Jack pulled over to the side of the road. He explains that in that split second of his near-catastrophe, he saw his life as a "medley of events leading to nowhere." Jack knew that he had been permanently changed in a fundamental way. The impact of the change had not, as yet, fully registered.

In an attempt to understand what had happened to him, Jack sought counseling from a therapist. He discovered that his drive to accumulate money had little to do with his family's happiness. In reality, they resented his time away from them. He realized how much time he spent devising ways of getting more money from insurance companies and government agencies that sometimes bordered on falsifying his services. In spite of how much money he earned, it was being spent faster than he could accumulate it. He also realized that his credit cards were always overextended. This situation required "creative" ways of manipulating money that were at the least unethical, and probably illegal. As he replayed the "medley of events" of his life, Jack had a profound realization. He realized that his drive to make more money was a game without end. That is, *he needed to own all the money that existed in order to be secure!* In spite of the impossibility of his accomplishing this unreasonable task, that is what Jack actually believed at a subconscious level. This belief is what drove him. The underlying "aha" that led to his experience of humility was the realization that beneath it all, he was actually attempting to achieve "absolute security."

Through his personal insight, Jack learned that absolute security does not exist, no matter how much money is accumulated. His insecurity, stemming from a poverty-stricken childhood, could never be satiated by earning more money—thus his symbolic realization of "a medley of events leading to nowhere." Jack describes this realization as having shaken the foundation of his entire existence. Everything changed.

What is Jack's life like today? Following his realization, he immediately dropped the clinic work. He also began to view his patient/doctor relationship as one of changing roles. He would sometimes be the doctor of physical ailments, but often he was also the patient as he learned about life from his clientele. Whatever illusions he had previously believed about his being superior were invalidated. *The experience of equality is the essence of humility.* Jack also began conversations with his family about his realizations and how he had changed. These conversations were, at first, very upsetting to the family since they had enjoyed a worry-free life so far as money was concerned. But now, Jack was breaking the unspoken agreement they shared: he earned the money and they told him how happy they were—which is the same as how secure they felt. This confrontation with his family's expectations continues to be the most challenging aspect of Jack's transformation. Will the family be willing (as opposed to *able*) to accept and adjust to Jack's transformation? At the time of this writing, the issue had not been resolved.

For Jack, his immediate sphere of responsibility is his family and his medical practice. He transformed the nature of both as a result of his own transformation. It is clear to Jack that much of his life's activity is now driven by an inner desire to contribute to the physical well-being of others. He describes his inner desire as spiritual. He makes the point that spirituality is not to be confused with altruism, which he feels is driven from a *belief* in doing good for others. Belief-driven behaviors generally have a personal motivation, such as acknowledgment in service to others. To be spiritually driven is to discover your life's purpose and to fully express it, whether acknowledged or not. This *natural* desire to serve and contribute to others transcends beliefs and expectations that are personally motivated. It is based upon an unconditional commitment that is driven from one's inner spiritual self.

Service Is an Unconditional Commitment

A basic premise for serving is being *unconditionally* committed to the growth, success, and well-being of others. An unconditional commitment means that there are no stated or unstated expectations as a motivation for contributing to someone's success. As suggested in the previous section, true service is not altruistic—where altruism carries any form of subtle or overt personal expectation. Such a commitment is born from the realization of our natural connectedness to others. It is our human differences that tend to create the idea of distinctions and, correspondingly, separateness. But, from a spiritual perspective, separateness is an illusion with respect to relationship.

For example, if I were to hide the palm of my hand such that you only saw four different-sized fingers and a thumb, distinct, separate digits would appear to be real. However, when I reveal my hand and you see that my fingers and thumb are actually fundamentally connected by the palm of my hand, we begin to understand that all five digits are inextricably related. In fact, it is only through this connectedness that fingers and thumb work together to perform essential functions, such as writing this book. In a like manner, a basic necessity for serving is realizing the natural connectedness we have with those whom we serve in a business capacity.

In business transactions, unconditionality is put into practice *after* a contractual agreement is established. Instead of simply fulfilling the letter of a contract, both parties flexibly transact in a way that is mutually beneficial. Furthermore, each party commits to 100% responsibility for the success of the other. It is not a 50/50 commitment! Assuming 100% responsibility for the success of someone else encourages extraordinary support in behalf of that individual, particularly when unexpected. This level of commitment has the greatest probability for mutual success. The following story illustrates these statements.

"I'm Bill Harrelson, VIP"

Li Ming is an airline ticket agent who works at the busy Chicago O'Hare Airport for one of the major airlines. Li is a second generation Chinese-American. Her family values are strongly rooted in the philosophy of Lao-Tzu, a sixth century B.C. Chinese philosopher and the founder of Taoism. Therefore, compassion, patience, and the understanding of others are considered virtues in her family.

Bill Harrelson was scheduled on a business trip from San Francisco to Rochester, New York. Just before leaving San Francisco, he learns of the death of a close relative in Detroit, Michigan. When he arrives in Chicago, he goes to the ticket counter where Li is serving customers. Bill impatiently informs her that he would like to be rerouted to Detroit for three days and then proceed to Rochester. He also indicates that the change is due to a death in his family which qualifies him for a discounted ticket to Detroit. Li listens patiently to Bill's situation, which takes about five minutes for him to explain. During this time, Bill does not notice the subtle signs of empathy and compassion displayed by Li because of a recent death in her own family. Meanwhile, those passengers in line behind Bill become noticeably irritated, assuming that the resolution of his situation is going to be lengthy. As a result of their reaction, Bill begins to project *his* discomfort onto Li, targeting her as the source of the problem.

Li patiently explains to Bill that she cannot issue a discounted ticket without proof of death, the name of the funeral home, and prior notice of the request that had been approved by her supervisor. Bill becomes incensed. He asks her how could she expect him to have such information and approval on such short notice. He further informs her that he is a million-mile flyer on their airline and that he deserves some form of special consideration in this situation. During his tirade, Bill informs Li of the name of his deceased relative, who had lived in one of the Detroit suburbs. Li asks Bill's forgiveness and informs him that she has to consult her supervisor in order to obtain the clearance he requests. She also calls another agent to assist with the passengers in her line while she consults with her supervisor.

Li goes into her supervisor's office to place a call to Bill's family in the Detroit suburbs and obtains the required information. She then returns to the ticket counter and informs him that his discounted ticket has been cleared and issues it to him. She smiles shyly and apologizes for the time it took to get the clearance and says that she hopes that things will go as well as possible in Detroit. For the first time, Bill recognizes the empathy and compassion in Li's expression. He smiles broadly, thanks her, and makes a mental note of the name on her badge.

Postscript: Bill Harrelson was influential in his own right. The Vice President of Administrative Services for the airline was a good friend of his. As a result of Bill's feedback about the service he received from Li Ming, she was immediately advanced to a supervisory position. Li now also conducts seminars for ticket agents on how to remain poised in stressful situations. Thus, the spiritual saying: "What goes around, comes around."

The Learning—Making an unconditional commitment to someone is the result of experiencing *empathy*, *compassion*, *humility*, and *love*. These are defined below:

- *Empathy* is the true caring and understanding of another's path as if it were your own; to *be* and *see* the world through their eyes.

- *Compassion* is the unconditional acceptance of how others have chosen to create the circumstances of their lives and, where appropriate, have them realize the potential they possess for change.

- *Humility* is the *realization* of the inherent equality of all human beings irrespective of differences, achievements, station in life, or any and all measures used to create distinctions.

- *Love* is the realization of the interconnectedness we have with each other and the wisdom to know that, in conflict situations, we are observing mirror images of ourselves.

As you read these definitions, you can see how each of them was played out in Li Ming's experience with Bill Harrelson. By the time their encounter was concluded, Li Ming had significantly impacted Bill's sense of appreciation for someone exposed to continual pressure.

Continuous Learning—Quality Improvement, Creativity, and Innovation

A spiritually sourced mind-set of service is translated into practical application in proportion to the education, skills, and competencies we each possess. Because of the continually changing needs and desires of those we serve, service is dynamic. This means that we must continually upgrade our competencies as our customers' needs and desires change. Today's emphasis on diversity has created special challenges in terms of reconciling speed, costs, and customized products and services.

For example, as information systems and technology continue to proliferate, personal computer (PC) users have a tremendous variety of needs. These needs span the range from administrative, to computer-assisted design and manufacturing (CAD and CAM), to multimedia capabilities. Therefore, designing a system of production that effectively takes into account marketing and sales, research and development, manufacturing, distribution, and cost administration can be a formidable task for a PC manufacturer. Inspired by this challenge, Hewlett-Packard (HP) developed an integrated system of production that was acknowledged in 1996 as "best in class" in meeting not only the diverse needs of customers, but also the retailers who sell their products. When HP decided to develop a single hard drive to accommodate both DOS and MAC operating systems, they also saved their retailers valuable shelf space and inventory. In 1999, *Windows Magazine* rated HP excellent in system reliability, service, and tech support. *PC Magazine*, in a like manner, gave HP an "A" and "Reader's Choice" for service and reliability. As discussed in Chapter One,

HP's heritage is creativity and innovation, not only in products and services, but also in process reengineering.

Therefore, the first stage of customer service is meeting or exceeding those needs or expectations that are obvious or obtained from direct customer feedback. These efforts might be categorized as Continuous Quality Improvement (CQI). For those organizations that are equally driven in terms of service, their Research and Development (R&D) departments are continually seeking ways to measurably improve a product or service beyond the immediately apparent needs of the clientele. This process is initiated by acquiring user information from product service centers and by marketing and sales' continual contact with customers after a sale is made. This information is then used to give direction to R&D in their efforts to *create* and *innovate* the next generation product or service. The next step in this process involves creatively integrating the information received, along with ongoing research, to actually *produce* the next generation product or service. It is important to note that this product or service cannot be described by customers since they are usually unaware, as yet, that they need it. This process is illustrated by the challenge Iomega faced in the early 1990s.

Customers—The Source of Change

Iomega Corporation is a Salt Lake City-based organization that produces portable data storage hardware—the Bernoulli box. Over a period of 13 years, they improved this product principally on the basis of internal research efforts by their in-house engineers. As sales began to decline, they came to the conclusion that they had about eight months before going out of business unless something dramatic occurred in terms of new product development. Dramatic change began when they hired a new CEO who, in turn, brought on board a new vice president of marketing two months later.

The organization began an extensive customer feedback program. They also conducted customer focus groups to discover what customers needed and wanted, and what users thought of their present product. The organization received valuable feedback about the design of their product. They discovered that the customer wanted a storage drive that was simple to use, required little space, and an accompanying user manual that did not require an engineering degree to understand. This feedback turned out to be invaluable for Iomega's engineers and designers. It provided the opportunity for them to reinvent the company around a customer-driven strategy. In response, Iomega produced their revolutionary new product, the Zip drive. They referred to the stored data as "stuff" and simplified the design in accordance with the recommendations of their focus groups.

If you are guessing that this is a success story about turning a company around in terms of revenue, your guess is right. Those are, after all, primarily the examples we use in our books. In this case, Iomega's revenues in 1991 were $136 million. During the one-year period from 1994 to 1995, they went from a $141 million to a $326 million company (an over 100% increase), and in 1996 their revenues were in excess of $1 billion. In 1998, the company achieved even greater financial success. What we learn from this story is that monetary success is often the result of a transformation in an organization's mind-set relating to service, commonly referred to as reinventing the company. However, new products have limited lifetimes, so their generation is an endless process. The necessary ingredients for an organization's continuing success are *anticipating* customers' needs and creating products and services that *exceed* their expectations.

Any Quantum-Thinkers in the House?

There are organizations that are in a class of their own where service is concerned. These are organizations that view themselves as *forging* the future. They have already learned to anticipate the next paradigm and generate the corresponding products and services. Initially, these products and services have little relationship to what customers believe they need or want. Quite often, the introduction of such a product or service is initially met with suspicion and doubt, or with outright resistance. This product or service seeks to redefine the assumptions or working principles of the existing paradigm. Therefore, the new product or service appears to be a threat to those attached to the present paradigm.

Historically, we can see these statements played out in retrospect. Moving from hunting, foraging, and wandering (which spanned centuries), the paradigm that redefined living groups of that era was based upon agriculture. Thus, domesticated animals, farming, farm utensils, and seedlings became the commodities of business. In this paradigm, power was based upon land ownership. The Agricultural Age lasted about 10,000 years. The next major paradigm began in England in the mid-1600s and is described as the Industrial Revolution. Many of the innovations of that era revolutionized the U.S.

economy. This paradigm is also attributed, in part, to dividing the agricultural South and the industrial North, as a significant factor that resulted in the Civil War. The locomotive was one of the major inventions in land transportation during this era. The Industrial Age roughly spanned the years 1650 to 1950 (a period of just 300 years). Power during this era was based upon capital or money. Around the mid-1900s, the Information Age began. The major event of this era was the invention of machines called computers that could efficiently store, retrieve, and process information. This paradigm lasted from about 1950 to 1990 (a period of only 40 years). Power, in this more recent age, was based upon information needed in making strategic business decisions.

Overlapping the Information Age is the Knowledge-based Age. Computers are products of the Information Age and software programs are products of the Knowledge-based Age. The latter paradigm began about 1985 and will run to about the year 2000 (a mere 15-year period). Power in this age is based upon knowledgeable, competent people. For example, seven of the top ten earners in the National Football League are quarterbacks, not because they are more skilled athletes, but because the position is more knowledge-based than *possibly* any of the others on the team. In this paradigm, emphasis is placed on creating "new knowledge" that continually produces, in turn, new products, services, and ways to be successful.

Although the various paradigms have time spans of dominance, they never go out of existence. That is, land, capital, information, and knowledge all play critical roles in successful organizations today. They are used in varying combinations, depending on the type of business enterprise.

The key to discovering your future product or service is being able to predict the next paradigm. This ability is called quantum-thinking. Having identified the next paradigm, you might ask, "What is our unique product or service that corresponds to this paradigm?" Credible responses require individuals who are unrestricted, "out-of-the-box" thinkers. It may also be necessary to predict succeeding paradigms since their time frames, as shown in the foregoing discussion, are rapidly decreasing. For example, if the present paradigm, which began in the mid-1990s, is Spirituality (which is overlapping the decline of the Knowledge-based paradigm), "what product or service could you create that would be the result of spiritual sourcing *and* have practical application in everyday life?" Great question, right? Suppose the next paradigm after Spirituality is Oneness or Unity—that is, the planetary realization that separateness is an illusion (e.g., the global internet). What would be your new product or service? After all, the *onset* of this paradigm has already begun!

Discontinuous Learning—Quantum-Thinking

Quantum-thinking is the ability to access an expanded level of consciousness, *beyond* creativity and imagination. This ability is acquired through an *in-depth* process of personal transformation. The process involves the invalidation of a major self-limiting belief an individual has about his or her ability to freely explore their creative consciousness. The invalidation of this self-limiting belief is the breakthrough to quantum-thinking. Examples of products resulting from quantum-thinking breakthroughs are the transitions from the vacuum tube to the transistor, the calculator to the computer, vinyl records to compact disks, and instructional learning to interactive transformational learning. The more we are "firmly attached" to the fundamental principles of a presently existing paradigm, the less the breakthrough experience is available. As Pablo Picasso stated:

"The act of creation
is simultaneously the
act of destruction."

Typical examples of self-limiting beliefs are: "The earth is stationary and the center of the universe;" "The earth is flat;" "If God had meant for man to fly, he would have given him wings;" "Cold fusion does not exist;" "Molecules do not have consciousness;" "Science is the study of reality;" and "Psychic powers are not real." These all comprise self-imposed limitations that prevent new concepts or paradigms of thinking from becoming reality. Quantum-thinking is achieved by the development of six critical skills. These skills must be mastered in addition to the invalidation of one's self-limiting belief discussed above. The six skills are:

1. *Personal Mastery*—the achievement of self-actualization and a high level of professional competency.

2. *Creative Synthesis*—the ability to transform information into new knowledge.

3. *Intuition*—the ability to acquire and validate spontaneous insights which are not rationally derived.

4. *Context Integration*—the ability to *see* the relationship between information in several contexts and

integrate those contexts to produce a new higher-order context.

5. *Hyper-accelerated Information Processing*—the ability of the mind to process data and information at hyper-accelerated speeds.

6. *Mastery of Context*—the ability to see the "big picture" from the fragment parts, by functioning at a level beyond a given paradigm.

Organizations that develop these six critical skills create what is genuinely described as a competitive advantage. Their major focus is not on competing, but continually creating the next paradigm products and services. The overall strategic focus is to be "beyond competition" by establishing the industry standard. These organizations are sometimes referred to as pioneers rather than settlers. A critical characteristic of a Living Organization is its ability to produce a unique product or service beyond the conventional wisdom of the industry that appeals to a mass market of customers.

Organizations that have exemplified quantum-thinking include: Southwest Airlines, Microsoft, Compaq, Disney, and Boeing. Southwest is considered to be the premier low-cost airline appealing to a mass market. It offers no frills, but exceptionally safe operation, outstanding customer service, and is the hands-down winner of on-time departures and arrivals. Microsoft took the software industry by storm in the 1980s and has continued to spin-off new related software products and services. It has also established a successful global network. Compaq's initial success was its IBM-compatible PC that dominated the market, even over IBM. Compaq reinvented themselves again in the late 1980s with their SystemPro server designed to run on five network operating systems: OS/2, Vines, Netware, SCO UNIX, and DOS. Their success continues with updated servers and a focus on customer services.

Disney is *the* classic business entertainment success story, beginning with movie animation products, expanding into theme parks, retail stores and, most recently, into television ownership for achieving expanded distribution. After its early days, Boeing bet the company on the success of the 707, which turned out to be a huge success. This success was followed by the 727 and projected into a unique category with the creation of the 747 jumbo jet. The 777 is a continuing quantum jump by Boeing, both in its partnership with suppliers and customers working together to design the aircraft, as well as in its use of computer technology for flying the aircraft.

What all of these examples have in common is that when a paradigm shift is made, it involves new product/service development, vastly improved customer service, or a vastly expanded distribution process. Such a shift also involves discontinuous, out-of-the-box learning that *anticipates* what customers want and what they will eventually need. As mentioned previously, these are typically products or services that the customer could not request of a provider in advance. Additional examples of such paradigm-breaking products include the microwave oven, fax machine, E-mail, CD player, and cellular telephone.

In Search of Service

Ultimately, service results in customers experiencing growth, success, and a sense of well-being. They additionally experience a feeling of being contributed to in a way that affects or even transforms their lives. Since transformation is always reciprocal, the provider also experiences a sense of being contributed to beyond remuneration. When transformation occurs, we experience an expanded understanding of ourselves and others that is described as wisdom.

The following are stories about friends and myself where we believe something "heartfelt" occurred in the process of service being rendered.

Cash Is Not Good Enough: A friend of mine, Phil, who is a frequent business traveler, checked into a Marriott hotel. He chose to pay cash for a two-night stay. He was informed by the desk clerk that he could not have a mini-bar key because he did not check in with a credit card. The desk clerk indicated the reason for this policy was that there was no way to ensure payment of what he would use from the mini-bar. Phil informed the clerk that he had left his credit cards at home and wondered if his prepayment might serve as security. The agent said, "No." When Phil got to his room he called the hotel manager and related what had happened. The manager came to his room immediately, refunded his two-day prepayment, and provided him with a key to the mini-bar. The manager then said, "My sincere apologies from Marriott Hotel; your stay is on us." To this day, Phil exclusively lodges at Marriott if at all possible.

Changing Gates: Fred travels around the world giving seminars on time management and high performance. While waiting for a Southwest Airlines flight from Salt Lake City to Los Angeles, Fred decided to do a little shopping since there was a fair amount of time available before his scheduled departure. Upon returning from shopping shortly before takeoff, Fred discovered that the departure gate was changed. He had not heard any gate changes over the public address system, so he naturally assumed that his flight would be leaving from the originally scheduled gate. He also realized that he had timed his return so close that he could not make it to the reassigned gate before his flight's departure. The agent at the gate where the flight was originally scheduled apologized profusely. Fred indicated that missing the flight was his responsibility and asked how he might get rescheduled on the next available plane to Los Angeles. The gate agent was so accustomed to customers berating him for such occurrences that he was surprised by Fred's ownership for the mishap. As a result, the agent gave Fred a free round trip ticket on Southwest and offered to help him with local Los Angeles transportation in the event he needed a rental car. To this day, Fred loves and regularly uses Southwest Airlines.

Where Is the Package?: A small business in Salt Lake City was awaiting an important business contract to be delivered by UPS. The contract involved an agreement that had to be signed that day before midnight. When the business owner had not received the package by 3:00 P.M., he called UPS tracking to locate it. Gary, the UPS driver, was contacted via dispatch by the business owner. Gary relayed that he did not have the package among his deliveries. At first the business owner was extremely upset. Then he settled down and explained to Gary how important the package was to his company. After completing his regular deliveries at 9:00 P.M. that night, Gary went back to central dispersing and searched through more than five hundred packages to find the one sent to the small business. He then delivered it to the business owner's home. As a result, the owner was able to sign the contract and have it notarized before midnight. The owner of the company was extremely grateful for the level of service rendered by Gary. In response, the owner wrote a glowing letter to UPS, expressing his gratitude for Gary's actions. Gary subsequently won the UPS Annual Service Award.

The Miracle of Birth: I had practiced for several weeks as the coach for the birth of our daughter, Lea. The obstetrician, Cynthia Jones, was an exceptionally sensitive woman who exuded professional confidence. Given years of experience, obstetricians have determined how to wait until the last minute before arriving at the hospital for a delivery. The attending nurses who were assisting in the process of Lea's delivery had the patience of Job. My anxiety focused on the onset of dilation, which I was told was the cue for delivery. Within an interval of ten minutes, my wife, Linda, went from four to eight centimeters. The nurse immediately phoned Cynthia, who said she would be right over—as if she were dropping by for a drink or a chat. When she arrived, all was in readiness and the staff responded with visible respect and professionalism. As coach, I had assumed that my job was to keep harmony among the team, but since everyone else had something to do, I felt extremely superfluous. Cynthia suggested that I assist her by helping my wife with her breathing sequence.

Whether she was just giving me something to do, or genuinely needed my help, I did appreciate being an *active* part of the delivery team. My wife and I had guessed that the baby would be a girl since, according to Cynthia's conventional wisdom, active babies are girls, while boys are laid back and expect things to be done for them.

As it turned out, Cynthia was right. Lea made her debut into this reality at 1:30 A.M. on September 20, 1993. The experience transformed me permanently. The entire staff cried. We had all experienced the miracle of birth—a truly spiritual experience—together. Thank you, Cynthia, and thank you, Holy Cross Hospital of Salt Lake City, Utah. The care, support, and love provided by Cynthia, the hospital staff, and the delivery team is still part of the indelible experience of my daughter's birth.

All of these stories are examples of outstanding customer service. When someone does something spontaneously that not only serves an individual, but also touches the heart, it is spiritually sourced. The truth is, it is an act of love, although most of us might be too embarrassed to admit it.

Jan Carlzon, former CEO of Scandinavian Airlines System (SAS), calls these situations "moments of truth"—those unplanned "opportunities in disguise" that are motivated from the heart and lead us to exceed the expectations of customers. Responding from the heart cannot be taught by a quality or service course. Such a response comes naturally to someone who has validated and integrated spirituality into their daily functioning. Dedicated ways of learning this way of being are discussed in the following chapter on self-awareness.

The questionnaire on the following pages can be used to evaluate the quality of service you provide to your customers, inquire whether a "human touch" was experienced by your customers, and to possibly update your job description.

Service Performance Evaluation

This questionnaire is designed to assist you in evaluating your service to internal and external customers.

Employee Self-Evaluation

Who are my three (3) primary customers? (Who is most affected by my competence to do my job and my commitment to quality service?)

Internal	External
1)	1)
2)	2)
3)	3)

What do my primary customers expect of me? (Stated and unstated).

Internal	External
1)	1)
2)	2)
3)	3)

Customer Feedback

Am I below, meeting, or exceeding my primary customers' expectations based upon their feedback, corresponding to each category on the preceding page?

Internal	External
1) ☐ Below ☐ Meets ☐ Exceeds Explain:	1) ☐ Below ☐ Meets ☐ Exceeds Explain:
2) ☐ Below ☐ Meets ☐ Exceeds Explain:	2) ☐ Below ☐ Meets ☐ Exceeds Explain:
3) ☐ Below ☐ Meets ☐ Exceeds Explain:	3) ☐ Below ☐ Meets ☐ Exceeds Explain:

Schedule a meeting with your three (3) primary customers to discuss *their* expectations and your personal evaluation of how well you are serving them.

After completing the above, define (or redefine) your job description on the following page.

This question is to be completed by your customer.

The Human Touch – Did you experience a "human touch" beyond job expectations, in the way my responsibilities were performed?
  Yes   No   If yes, please comment.

Job Description (defined or redefined)

1.

2.

3.

4.

5.

Organizational Self-Awareness— Know Thyself

"Since all creation is a whole, separateness is an illusion. Like it or not, we are all team players."

The Tao of Leadership
John Heider

Introduction

Self-awareness is an *in-depth* understanding of one's self that is the result of personal growth. Personal growth is the lifelong process of learning by experience. It commonly occurs when we encounter an interpersonal conflict that requires us to irreversibly change. This process is called transformation. Transformation that restructures our reality or redefines our value system is spiritual.

For example, the experience of a "mid-life crisis" results in spiritual transformation and greater self-awareness. We become more skilled at resolving difficulties we encounter. Mastery of self is a necessity for understanding and being sensitive to the difficulties others experience. Hence, the saying, "I cannot facilitate in others what I have not mastered in myself." The average sum of employee self-awareness is defined as organizational self-awareness. It is measured by the extent to which interpersonal conflict is minimized in an organization's overall operation.

This chapter will discuss how the interpersonal dynamics in your organization (and your life) either drain your energy and spirit or are an incredible source of power that propels you in achieving your personal and professional aspirations.

Interpersonal Relationships

Author Peter Koestenbaum has estimated that 80% of the "loss processes" in organizations are actually due to dysfunctional interpersonal dynamics.[8] As organizations continue to become more relationship-focused through teamwork and other high-involvement processes, the potential for loss in productivity can increase exponentially. An accountant can easily calculate bottom line losses due to process breakdown, conflict, repetition, delays, etc. On the other hand, the committed alignment of people to achieving an objective can create synergy that increases productivity two or threefold.

In spite of the loss processes cited above, we pretend that interpersonal dynamics have no *direct* relationship to profit and loss. We refer to them as "soft skills," as if to imply they are of no bottom line value in the "hard" world of business. I suspect we use these arguments as an attempt to avoid the genuine examination of ourselves. We tend to embrace expressions like "don't focus on people, focus on the process." However, in terms of interpersonal dysfunction, we *are* the problem. More specifically, our attitudes, beliefs, and corresponding behaviors are *exactly* the source of our interpersonal conflicts—not processes or procedures. This is particularly true where diversity issues are concerned, and it's time we began telling the truth. The following example illustrates the interpersonal conflict self-managed teams inevitably encounter, particularly when there are ethnic, gender, and cultural diversity issues to deal with.

Self-Managed Teams Require a Rite of Passage

A large manufacturing firm in the Midwest delegated authority to several of its successfully-managed production units to extensively implement teaming. One team, consisting of several highly empowered individuals, decided they wanted to attempt a stretch project. The project involved reduction of the fabrication cycle time of sensitive machinery components by one-half. If successful, this breakthrough could save the company about $100 million annually. The team was given the go ahead to operate as independently as possible. They had worked together for so long that they assumed the major obstacles to their success would be technical and process problems. The team consisted of Larry, Ken, Lori, Jeffrey, Marlene, Ali, and Murray.

The signs of tension began when they attempted to decide how they would organize and administer the team's operation. Larry suggested that Ken, who was a supervisor, be the team leader. Lori, who had really never gotten along with Ken, disagreed. As an equal team member, she felt free for the first time to express her discomfort with Ken. She felt that Ken believed that women who had young children should be at home with them. She indicated that he was a member of a religious group that espoused such beliefs.

At first, Ken felt defensive, stating that he was able to separate his religious beliefs from how he managed people at work. Jeffrey, an African-American team member, stated that Ken was fooling himself if he believed that he could change simply because he crossed the doorway of the workplace. The other female member of the team, Marlene, stated that she had not experienced any instances of discrimination from Ken. She felt it was counterproductive to attack him. She also suggested they focus on the project and not on people or personalities. Then she turned to Ali and asked him for his opinion regarding the accusation being made about Ken. Marlene did not notice that Ali felt embarrassed about being placed in this situation. He was uncomfortable about the open criticism of others. This type of situation is called "violating face" in the culture in which he was raised. After looking at the floor for what seemed like an eternity, given the tension in the room, Ali finally stated softly, "I think we should be willing to discuss any issue that someone feels is valid and important to our team's success. After all, the entire organization is expecting us to be successful in this project."

Everyone looked at Murray for his input. He had been with the organization for thirty-five years and had seen initiatives come and go. But this time, he felt something different was happening. He felt the leadership *had* to change their way of operating or the company would soon be out of business. This was the first time he felt there was a genuine opportunity to actually shift power to employees, and it would be a shame if the team failed.

The team decided to put aside discussions of technical and process functions until their interpersonal issues were resolved. They held several three-hour sessions with a skilled facilitator where gut-wrenching issues of religion, sexism, racism, ageism, and ethnocentrism were discussed. In these sessions anger, defen-

siveness, emotionalism, crying, introspection, and transformation all took place. By going through this process,
each of the team members realized that their own personal prejudices were, in fact, the source of the discord
they were experiencing as a team. As they were each
facilitated through the Elisabeth Kübler-Ross process of
denial, reaction, bargaining, guilt, and *acceptance,*[5] the
team members also realized that the issues discussed
were latent in each of them. They also came to understand that, if ignored, these issues would eventually
resurface in some other counterproductive way. Furthermore, they realized that it is only through nonresis-
tant acceptance that one is freed to *be* and *behave* in a
manner that respects the dignity of others. This realization, by an individual or a group, is their confirmation of
having achieved "the rite of passage" characterized by
the Elisabeth Kübler-Ross process.

This process took about a month. In the end, a self-
managed team began to emerge. It was acknowledged
that Ken was best qualified to lead the team to a place
where leadership roles would rotate. They also realized
that the technical aspects of the project were easy as
compared to what they each experienced personally.
They proceeded to creatively redesign the fabrication process using the full range of the team's talents since there
was little interpersonal conflict to deal with. Solving
the cycle-time puzzle was simultaneously challenging
and fun. However, they continued to use the facilitator
throughout the duration of the project as a preventative
measure. This process of integrating humanistic practices as a natural part of a team's operation is an example of spirituality in the workplace.

The Golden Rules for Self-Managed Teams

The golden rules for self-managed teams, that we learn from the previous example, are the following:

1. Each team member must be technically competent in his or her unique role.

2. Each team member must learn team management skills for effective team administration.

3. Each team member must accept 100% responsibility and accountability for his or her unique role, *and* simultaneously, accept 100% responsibility and accountability for the team's success.

4. During the process of becoming self-managing, each team member *must* be willing to confront and resolve his or her own interpersonal issues or possibly leave the team as a result of an unwillingness to confront such issues.

5. In the case of diverse, cross-cultural teams, each team member must confront and resolve programmed prejudices, biases, and ethnocentrism as a necessity for participation and team success.

6. Issues of diversity will overshadow the effective implementation of high-performance teaming and *force* us to deal with them. If we don't deal with these issues, teamwork will fail; high performance will fail; and the organization will fail!

In summary, there are three major requirements for a self-managed team: technical competence, management administration, and self-mastery.

The Global Challenge

From a global perspective, business transactions with most organizations of the non-Western world are based upon a firm foundation of interpersonal trust through quality relationships. These global relationships are more challenging than domestic issues since they also involve fundamental differences in cultural values. Fundamental societal values of the non-Western world that are integrated into their business functioning include group, face (i.e., respect for the dignity of others), loyalty, and obligation to others. In the Western world, we tend to value individuality, personal achievement, and commitment to self. These differences must be reconciled in order to have successful, long-term business relationships.

Organizations that are self-aware understand how interpersonal relationships either contribute to or detract from their success. They take whatever steps are necessary to inform their employees why addressing such sensitive issues are in their best interests as well as the best interests of the organization. In summary, the quality of an organization is the sum of the quality of its interpersonal relationships. Relationship and communication are inseparable as we discover in the following section.

Interpersonal Communication

Communication is the expression of relationship. That is, whatever we *do* in relationship with others is communication. Therefore, communication can be verbal, nonverbal, emotional, subliminal, or even spiritual. Verbal and nonverbal communications are rather obvious aspects of communication with which we are familiar. Emotional communication involves the expression of feelings such as happiness, joy, neutrality, anger, or depression. Subliminal communication involves an underlying intent of which we may be unaware. That is, we *say* one thing and *do* another. The model of subliminal communication is illustrated below.

Subliminal Communication Model

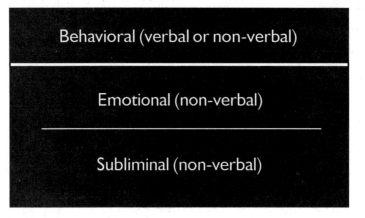

Behavioral (verbal or non-verbal)

Emotional (non-verbal)

Subliminal (non-verbal)

Behavioral communication is what is stated or implied non-verbally. It is direct, not emotional or subliminal, e.g., speaking, touching, gestures, body language, etc.

Emotional communication is determined by how we *experience* each other. It is an expression of our *emotional state*, e.g., enthusiasm, joy, neutrality, anger, or fear. Behavioral and emotional communication are obviously coupled.

Subliminal communication is based on what we *believe* and *value*. It is often an expression of what we truly *intend* to happen. All three forms of communication occur simultaneously.

For example, we may state that it is not our intention to have someone become upset as a result of a verbal exchange. However, if the consistent result we produce is that the other person *is* upset then, at some level, that is the communication we intend. This is called subliminal communication. A particularly undermining form of this communication is gossip. Gossip not only undermines an individual's reputation, but it also demoralizes the spirit of an organization.

Spiritual communication is the expression of relationship that "touches the soul." Spiritual communication is inspirational, whether the words are understood or not. Implicit in the expression of the words are intention, commitment, desire, and passion. For example, many of the speeches made by Dr. Martin Luther King Jr. contained very sophisticated words, phrases, and sentences that were probably beyond the comprehension of many in his listening audiences. However, this did not prevent them from "getting the message" or being inspired to march, sing, and tirelessly protest their conditions.

Spiritual Communication Is an Act of Inspiration

Spiritual communication has the power to cause transformation—whether it is a CEO communicating the vision, a line manager espousing empowerment, a mother teaching her child the virtues of sharing, or an individual operating in a courageous manner that influences the behavior of others. When transformation occurs, spirituality is an essential part of the transaction. We sometimes refer to individual demonstrations of courage as "acts of heroism." I prefer to call them "acts of inspiration" since this phrase acknowledges relatedness rather than individuality and separateness.

When Rosa Parks refused to give up her seat on a public bus to a white patron in Mobile, Alabama, in 1955, that was an act of inspiration. That incident sparked the Civil Rights Movement of the 1960s. When Gandhi decided to nonviolently protest the British occupation of India, that was an act of inspiration. When the president, CEO, or any employee actively practices humanistic values in the business environment, these are acts of inspiration. These actions are the nucleus that initiate the transformation of people, organizations, or societies. Whenever we take a stand for a spiritually sourced idea, no matter the magnitude of its impact, the action that follows is a spiritual communication. It is also important to remember that any such action is equal in importance to any that has occurred in the past or will occur in the future. *The impact of Gandhi, King, Schweitzer, or Mother Teresa is not of more or less importance than any "ordinary individual" who has similarly impacted the world in some small, unpublished way!*

Communication and Culture Are Inseparable

Where organizational awareness is concerned, communication and culture are inseparable. This statement is captured by the quote of Edward T. Hall:[9]

"Embedded in culture is communication;
and 90% of all communication is subliminal."

That is, the context that dictates "where one is coming from" is culturally based. From a global perspective, the cultural context of the Western world is low context. The cultural context of the non-Western world is high context. In low context cultures, the explicit verbal or written message carries the meaning. In high context cultures, that which is written or stated rarely carries the meaning. The meaning of the message is understood by reading between the lines for what is not written or stated. An example of how this difference can lead to miscommunication is described by the following story.

A funeral was held for an influential Mexican-American employee who had been employed by a major government facility in the Southwest. According to organizational policy, only immediate family members could be excused to attend a funeral during the work week. However, ten Mexican-American employees in the deceased individual's work unit indicated "they would like to attend the funeral." Their manager said he would think about their request. He forgot to respond to the employees in time, and they decided on their own to attend the funeral. Afterwards, the manager indicated he did not give them permission. The employees were perplexed and confused by his statement.

This incident led to a reexamination of the organization's policy regarding excused absences. In the process, the organization's management discovered that the employees' request to attend the funeral was more a "statement of intention" than it was a "request for permission." They were formerly indicating what they intended to do. To them, it was incomprehensible that the manager did not understand their request. In "extended family" cultures, like the Mexican-American culture, close friends *are* part of the immediate family. Unfortunately, the manager simply did not understand the communication "between the lines" and the nature of extended family cultures. Although the official policy of the agency did not change, it is now "flexibly" applied in practice. This example illustrates how communication and culture are inseparable.

Low context cultures include the U.S., Canada, England, Australia, Russia, and Northwestern Europe. High context cultures include China, Japan, Arabia, Mexico, South America, and the Pacific Islands. Countries that are in-between include France, Spain, Italy, Eastern Europe, and Greece. Low context cultures tend to be very verbal, whereas high context cultures tend to be less verbal or even nonverbal in communicating. It is not unusual to experience Japanese or Chinese individuals as "quiet." However, if one is sensitive to nonverbal cues such as eye movement, facial tension, and posture, it is possible to decipher an entire conversation with such a person with the least amount of verbalization. On the other hand, a conversation with someone from Greece, Spain, or Arabia might be very verbal and animated, but still the real messages are rarely explicitly stated. Therefore, in cultures like the U.S., there will be increasing potential for miscommunication unless we begin to acknowledge the importance of issues involving cross-cultural communication. Low context/high context global values and how they relate to workplace functioning will be discussed in more detail at the end of Chapter Seven.

Bridging Differences through Communication

Three phenomena that provide us the opportunity to bridge differences in cross-cultural communication are teamwork, diversity, and globalization. Both cross-functional and cross-cultural teams are designed to tap the synergy of different functional and cultural perspectives. Diversity seeks to validate the importance of differences as crucial to the profitable operation of an organization. Diversity can also be a continuing competitive advantage where such differences are creatively integrated into everyday business functioning. Globalization simply expands the size of the board upon which the game is played. From a U.S. perspective, its population composition is already a microcosm of the world. Globalization also significantly expands the spectrum of differences and *forces* the resolution of cross-cultural issues in order to have long-term mutually successful business transactions. Let's observe how communication breakdown occurs when cross-cultural communication styles are not recognized by a new product development team.

Cross-Cultural Communication in Teaming

A small business that produces and distributes educational programs for high school students anticipates the need for new product development. Their leadership decides they must consider the impact of information technology (IT) in terms of an updated delivery system. They organize a cross-functional team of six individuals representing research and development (R&D), strategic planning, marketing and sales, customer service, finance, and a long-term customer who is an education specialist.

Sherrie, the marketing and sales representative, informs the team that students like programs that are fast-moving, fun to play, and do not require too much thinking. Their teachers, on the other hand, are adamant about the content quality and learning potential of the new program series. Sherrie further explains that the challenge will be to satisfy the teachers, who will make the purchasing decision, *and* the students, who will be the end-users. "If the kids don't like the programs and don't use them, there will be no continuing purchases made anyway," Sherrie states. Margo, the education specialist, reaffirms the importance of content quality and learning. She informs the group that the state legislature had begun using standardized testing as the major measure of educational effectiveness and funding.

Each team member provided input from their perspective as the R&D staff began development of the new program. When Lee, from R&D, presented the first-stage program using CD-ROM technology, the team had varying opinions about the product. Margo liked the emphasis on learning content. Sherrie, from sales and marketing, felt the program was too linear, had little interactivity, and was not that much fun to use. She felt students would not be attracted to the program and would have to be forced to use it by teachers. Barry, the customer service representative, felt the program was not relevant to the needs of minorities. Robert, from finance, questioned whether they had prematurely gotten into a new activity that could bankrupt the company if they had guessed wrong in anticipating the future.

Lee, from R&D, explained that his department was aware of the present approach to CD-ROM programs in the consumer market. He explained that although consumer market products emphasized "lots of bells and whistles," there was little or no learning content. The team became polarized in their opinions and began levelling charges at each other of misunderstanding, "being stuck in the past," insensitivity, and a lack of trust and business focus. Most of the group were fearing that Robert might be correct about the inaccuracy of their business decision to "anticipate the future." Missing the mark on the first try can typically result in fear and a lack of constructive communication.

Wendy, from strategic planning, had simply observed everyone's reaction to the new CD-ROM program. When the heated exchanges had dissipated and a vacuum of quiet introspection replaced it, she asked if she might share her view of the situation. She indicated that her observation was that the performance of the "first-stage" program was not the problem. The problem was the way the team was *responding* to having not produced a perfect product on their first attempt. The fact that the organization was committed to computer learning was not a question of discussion. Wendy suggested that the problem was communication. She pointed out that some team members were focused on the task and business aspects while others were focused on how they were relating to each other. Without carefully listening to each other, they were missing the value of both. Integrating both points of view would be necessary to produce a successful product. Wendy also suggested that if the team could set aside the underlying fear of failure and realize the talent they each possessed, they would be able to effectively address the shortcomings of the first-stage program. Everyone agreed. In the days that followed they discovered that the ultimate solution to the apparent dilemma was to produce two products; one for group usage maximizing learning content and the other a single-user program with emphasis on choices, interactivity, and fun.

The Learning—What we learn from this example is that people and their technical competencies are rarely the source of interpersonal breakdown. The actual source is often the way we respond to each other when we experience conflict based upon an underlying fear. Each of us has either a relationship orientation or a task orientation in the way we communicate with each other. Neither is better than the other. *Relationship orientation* emphasizes trust, understanding, and sensitivity. *Task orientation* emphasizes roles, functions, and business strategy. The key to conflict resolution and synergy is learning to *integrate* the two orientations. Organizational self-awareness means that there is a sufficiently high level of employee perceptiveness that inevitable situations (like the previous example) are constructively and quickly resolved. Such perceptiveness is the result of personal and spiritual growth.

Personal and Spiritual Growth

Personal growth is the lifelong process of learning to distinguish between that which is real and that which is illusion. Illusions are those experiences we have programmed ourselves to believe are a threat to our physical survival, but in fact are not. An experience as simple as a disagreement about the best route to reach a destination can be perceived as threatening, if counterproductive emotions are aroused. The emotional upset we experience is personal feedback informing us that we are perceiving a threat from an opposing point of view. Reactions of this nature are traceable to some belief programmed in our view of reality. During a structured process, such as a training session or facilitated coaching, we gradually begin to learn that such beliefs are not valid.

For example, if an individual is motivated to perform in an exceptional manner as a result of constant positive acknowledgment, then he or she might have the following structured belief: "I am valued, appreciated, or worthy when acknowledged for what I achieve." An individual who has this belief will make major career decisions based upon the adequacy or lack of acknowledgment he or she continually receives. Eventually, this person will experience a confrontation where he or she learns, at least intellectually, that acknowledgment is not necessarily related to value, worth, or appreciation. Thus, the statement "the first step to change is awareness."

This person then becomes *consciously* aware of his or her pattern of setting up others for an expectation that can never be totally satisfied. That is, he or she realizes that there can never be sufficient external acknowledgment to validate his or her value, worth, or sense of appreciation. Particularly, since acknowledgments that are validating and sustaining must come from within. *The process of realizing a counterproductive pattern and letting go of the corresponding invalid belief, is personal growth.* Life appears to be a continual process of realizing and letting go. Some of us engage the process proactively. Whereas, many of us engage it resistantly as though we have to give up something that is essential for our survival. Wisdom involves the realization that personal growth is not a choice. We either experience it proactively or resistantly.

Spiritual growth is more challenging than personal growth, since it goes beyond the invalidation of a single belief. *Spiritual growth is the process of invalidating a system of beliefs that restructures our view of reality in a major way.* It is often the result of a "life-changing event" rather than a structured process. An example of this process is the spiritual transformation of Kofi Kwame.

The Spiritual Transformation of Kofi Kwame

Kofi Kwame is a first-generation Ghanaian from West Africa. He studied engineering at Georgia Institute of Technology. His family was very proud of his academic accomplishments. They emphasized to him that the key to *security* in life was to get a good education in a science or technical field. When Kofi chose engineering and excelled in his studies, it was like a dream come true for both him and his family. After acquiring his bachelor's and master's degrees in engineering, he was hired by a large chemical company in the midwestern U.S. He experienced exceptional success and rapid advancement. Eventually, he was assigned to a manager with whom he had a serious personality clash.

Kofi was now faced with his first major professional dilemma: remain where he was and hope that things would eventually work out for the better or ask to be transferred to a new division. Asking to be transferred would probably jeopardize his unblemished record. Remaining where he was, at least, ensured his security and probably a continued stellar career as long as he avoided any major clashes with his manager. Kofi struggled with this dilemma for a full year. The quality of his work began to suffer and his feelings of discontent began to earn him the reputation of a "possible trouble maker." His relationship with his family also deteriorated. He felt that any proactive steps he might take in resolving his dilemma—like going to his manager's superior—would not only threaten his career but, more importantly, his family's security as well.

Then Kofi met someone at an engineering conference who had a significant influence on his life. They established a close personal relationship. He suggested to Kofi that true security was the result of his ability to perform his work in an exceptional manner. And that such an ability comes from within. He also suggested that Kofi ask himself, "What would I like to do at this point in my life that would give me the greatest satisfaction?" The answer Kofi got was completely different from the one he had always planned—that of having a career with the company. He realized that what he really wanted to do was start a new business as a quality consultant. Although he knew nothing about running a business except what he had learned at his present company, Kofi was confident about his knowledge of engineering quality processes.

The most difficult part of his decision to change careers was not convincing his wife and two children, but his family in West Africa. They were not only vehemently opposed to the idea, but stated that, "they didn't even know what a consultant was! It certainly wasn't a secure profession like engineering." Because of family loyalty and respect, Kofi felt trapped by *their* expectations and beliefs about security.

In spite of the overwhelming pressures in opposition to his personal desire, Kofi left the company and started his own consulting business. He labored tirelessly for the first two years to ensure its success and establish its reputation. By small business standards, Kofi is now successful and earns an income about twice what his salary would have been at the chemical company. He has become comfortable with the freedom as well as the worries that come with a small business. He is also firmly convinced, at this point, that his security is within himself. This conviction was recently validated as he observed his friends from the chemical company either being laid off due to downsizing or offered early retirement packages. In fact, his friends describe him as having adopted a philosophical or somewhat mystical attitude toward life. Kofi feels that by letting go of "oughts" and "shoulds" from others, each one of us can tap into an internal guidance system if we are willing to listen to it. He calls this internal guidance system his still inner voice that constantly provides him wisdom and direction.

Human Potential, Like Consciousness, Is Unlimited!

What Kofi tapped into is "expanded consciousness." It is the source of inner wisdom. This domain goes beyond the finite definition we have of ourselves as separate and unique from others. Uniqueness is the result of how we individually view reality or organize our total accumulated knowledge. These descriptions are defined as one's personal consciousness as diagrammed in Figure 5 on the following page.

Figure 5. The sign ≡ means "is identical with," not "equal to."

The more we are attached to our view of reality, the less potential we have for unlimited creativity. Personal mastery is the process of "going beyond" the limited finite view we have of ourselves so as to access "expanded levels of consciousness"—also referred to as our creative consciousness as shown in Figure 6 on the following page.

The varying levels of consciousness represent varying levels of knowing as wisdom. Where wisdom is abundant in an organization, there is great self-awareness. Such an organization operates in an effective and efficient manner with the least amount of loss due to interpersonal conflict. This also means that all employees can operate in an unlimited manner whenever their job responsibilities require the use of their creative consciousness.

The dots in Figure 6 represent levels of consciousness beyond those shown, since consciousness is infinite in dimension. We are only limited by the self-imposed limitations of our own imagination!

Every time we "go inward" beyond our own personal consciousness, we access a level of expanded consciousness as shown in Figure 6. At the levels of ordinary and extraordinary problem-solving, we experience personal growth. When we consciously practice personal growth, spirituality becomes an integrated part of our everyday lives, influencing our moment-by-moment interpretation

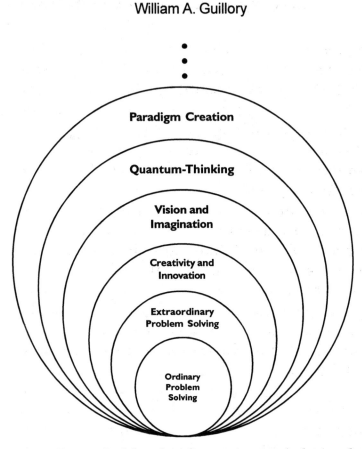

Figure 6. Expanded levels of consciousness beyond one's personal consciousness.

of life events as we experience them. Think of someone with whom you have an ongoing conflicting relation-ship—a relationship that triggers counterproductive feel-ings, emotions, and behaviors in you. If you were truly aware of the source of your reaction to this person, you probably would have permanently solved your continu-ing conflict. I don't mean fight or flight coping mecha-nisms, such as an unproductive confrontation or "get-ting rid of the person." I mean a serious examination of what *you* have to confront about yourself if you "let go" of your beliefs about that person. You may discover that the beliefs you have about that person are *possibly* true about you! Self-examination at this level opens you to the full capacity of your creative ability.

Creativity and innovation involve advances *within* a given paradigm. Examples are faster Pentium chips or new software programs. These are examples of advances *within* the Knowledge-based paradigm. Creativity and innovation are used to generate short-term business advantages. These abilities are absolute necessities for science, technology, and engineering-based organizations. Therefore, critical employees in these organizations must be able to routinely access this level of consciousness. And, correspondingly, they must be willing to pursue self-examination to at least the levels needed to establish the required capacity for such creative insights.

Vision and imagination demand more in terms of your ability to create beyond the base of knowledge. They require an ability to tap into the timeless state of consciousness where you can "envision the future." Envisioning involves experiencing a future state with your projected consciousness. For example, the United Nations—originally the League of Nations—was a vision of Woodrow Wilson, the 28th President of the United States. Putting a person on the moon by 1960 was the visionary challenge of President John F. Kennedy. A totally connected world through the use of the Internet was the vision of Tim Berners-Lee in 1991. It took nine years to crystallize his vision and another four years to convince others of its validity. Today, it is a reality with unlimited potential.

Expanding further into one's creative consciousness allows one to identify and even create new paradigms. This situation occurs when a vision is so ambitious that it also requires a major shift in human consciousness to be successful. Historical names associated with such paradigm shifts are Nicolaus Copernicus, Sigmund Freud, and René Descartes. Copernicus suggested that the sun was the center of the solar system, not planet Earth; Freud suggested the existence of the subconscious; and Descartes proposed rules for the objective study of science, separate and apart from religion or philosophy. When proposed and ultimately accepted, all three paradigms had a major shift in humankind's view of reality and how they functioned. A vision of human existence on the planet Earth where "peaceful co-existence is a way of life" will require a similar shift in human consciousness—which is the essence of the Spiritual paradigm. This shift will, of necessity, include the following spiritual principles:

1. We are all *inherently* equal as human beings.

2. Dignity, respect, and trust *voluntarily* govern our behavior.

3. We are each responsible and accountable for *every* condition on this planet.

4. This planet is *fully abundant* to support the needs of everyone.

5. We are *one* with all that exists.

These principles would guide, govern, and characterize our behaviors if we decided to minimize human conflict through personal and collective transformation.

An Organizational Context of Self-Awareness

A context of self-awareness exists where employees are encouraged to proactively engage in personal growth. Quality interpersonal dynamics are an ingrained part of the culture. When relationships are strained or the work requirements begin to create stress among employees, there is an expectation that such situations will be immediately resolved. In our work with organizations, we have found that employees consistently identify five major areas relating to the quality of interpersonal dynamics. They are *teamwork, relationship, trust, communication,* and *attitude.* We have also collected summarized descriptions from various organizations that define each of these characteristics.

Teamwork — Willing to work with others; interdependent; does not stand out; committed to team goals; understands the big picture; committed to others' success on the team; caring; and dedicated.

Relationship — Being honest; open; having integrity; being supportive; willing to listen; trusting; being kind; being genuine; showing respect; accepting of others; and having clear expectations.

Trust — Willing to keep agreements; being accountable; telling the truth; loving unconditionally; keeping things confidential; having integrity; having a sense of humor; being comfortable; and accepting of others.

Communication — Being direct; accurate; open; clear; non-manipulative; polite; candid; having no excuses; non-threatening; truthful; and assertive.

Attitude — Being positive; open; creative; realistic; caring; genuine; energetic; flexible; responsible; real; dedicated; going the extra mile; willing to try; persistent; serving; quality; eager; and global.

A self-aware organization is one that measures the quality of its interpersonal dynamics on a regular basis. In order to measure the quality of your organization's interpersonal dynamics, you might use the instrument on the following pages.

An Organizational Self-Awareness Instrument

An instrument used to measure the quality of the interpersonal dynamics of an organization is shown on the following pages. The instrument measures the perceptions employees have about each other in terms of *teamwork, relationship, trust, communication,* and *attitude*. Ideally, it can be used for work units, teams, or subgroups not exceeding twenty individuals. The size of a group is determined by the number of individuals in a work unit with sufficient contact to credibly evaluate each other.

There are four selections—Excellent (E), Very Good (VG), Good (G), and Poor (P)—for each of the five characteristics. For every good (G) or poor (P) circled, it is suggested that improvement is required. Therefore, summing all the good (G) and poor (P) selections for an individual gives a total score. The larger the total score, the more personal improvement is required. In addition, the total sums for each characteristic for an individual or the group provide valuable feedback for organizational improvement. As the total sums for individuals and the organization decrease, the organization becomes more self-aware. That is, the less the interpersonal conflict, the more an organization is self-aware.

The scores are usually tabulated by an independent outside individual (where necessary) and the feedback for each individual is confidentially given to that person. However, the total sums for each individual, in numerical order without names, are provided to each respondent. A blank instrument is shown on page 136, and a sample evaluation is shown on pages 137 through 140. Page 141 contains a more complete description of this testing and analysis process.

William A. Guillory

ORGANIZATIONAL SELF-AWARENESS

E = Excellent   VG = Very Good   G = Good   P = Poor

Name	Team Player	Relationship	Trust	Communication	Attitude
1)	E VG G P	E VG G P	E VG G P	E VG G P	E VG G P
2)	E VG G P	E VG G P	E VG G P	E VG G P	E VG G P
3)	E VG G P	E VG G P	E VG G P	E VG G P	E VG G P
4)	E VG G P	E VG G P	E VG G P	E VG G P	E VG G P
5)	E VG G P	E VG G P	E VG G P	E VG G P	E VG G P
6)	E VG G P	E VG G P	E VG G P	E VG G P	E VG G P
7)	E VG G P	E VG G P	E VG G P	E VG G P	E VG G P
8)	E VG G P	E VG G P	E VG G P	E VG G P	E VG G P
9)	E VG G P	E VG G P	E VG G P	E VG G P	E VG G P
10)	E VG G P	E VG G P	E VG G P	E VG G P	E VG G P
11)	E VG G P	E VG G P	E VG G P	E VG G P	E VG G P
12)	E VG G P	E VG G P	E VG G P	E VG G P	E VG G P
13)	E VG G P	E VG G P	E VG G P	E VG G P	E VG G P

ORGANIZATIONAL SELF-AWARENESS

E = Excellent   VG = Very Good   G = Good   P = Poor

Name	Team Player	Relationship	Trust	Communication	Attitude
1) Chin	E VG G P	E VG G P	E VG G P	E VG G P	E VG G P
2) Sherry	E VG G P	E VG G P	E VG G P	E VG G P	E VG G P
3) Sophia	E VG G P	E VG G P	E VG G P	E VG G P	E VG G P
4) Leroy	E VG G P	E VG G P	E VG G P	E VG G P	E VG G P
5) Juanita	E VG G P	E VG G P	E VG G P	E VG G P	E VG G P
6) Byron	E VG G P	E VG G P	E VG G P	E VG G P	E VG G P
7) Vladimir	E VG G P	E VG G P	E VG G P	E VG G P	E VG G P
8) Bessie	E VG G P	E VG G P	E VG G P	E VG G P	E VG G P
9) Mohammad	E VG G P	E VG G P	E VG G P	E VG G P	E VG G P
10) Daryl	E VG G P	E VG G P	E VG G P	E VG G P	E VG G P
11) Valerie	E VG G P	E VG G P	E VG G P	E VG G P	E VG G P
12) Karen	E VG G P	E VG G P	E VG G P	E VG G P	E VG G P
13) Raoul	E VG G P	E VG G P	E VG G P	E VG G P	E VG G P

ORGANIZATIONAL SELF-AWARENESS

E = Excellent   VG = Very Good   G = Good   P = Poor

Name	Team Player				Relationship				Trust				Communication				Attitude			
	E	VG	G	P	E	VG	G	P	E	VG	G	P	E	VG	G	P	E	VG	G	P
1) Chin	4	6	2	1	7	4	1	1	8	2	2	1	3	8	1	1	7	4	2	0
2) Sherry	5	7	1	0	7	4	2	0	6	5	1	1	7	6	0	0	8	4	1	0
3) Sophia	1	4	5	4	1	3	7	3	2	2	7	3	1	9	4	0	2	3	4	5
4) Leroy	7	5	1	0	4	7	2	0	9	4	0	0	5	6	2	0	6	4	3	0
5) Juanita	2	5	5	1	3	5	6	0	0	3	8	2	2	3	6	2	0	3	7	3
6) Byron	7	6	0	0	8	4	1	0	8	2	3	0	9	3	1	0	6	5	2	0
7) Vladimir	3	4	5	1	1	5	7	0	2	2	7	2	3	3	6	1	5	6	2	0
8) Bessie	3	8	2	0	4	6	1	0	7	5	0	1	6	5	2	0	9	3	1	0
9) Mohammad	4	6	3	0	4	5	3	1	7	4	2	0	2	2	9	0	9	4	0	0
10) Daryl	8	4	1	0	9	4	0	0	7	5	1	0	6	6	1	0	11	2	0	0
11) Valerie	5	6	1	1	4	4	3	2	5	5	2	1	5	7	1	0	5	5	2	1
12) Karen	5	8	1	0	6	7	0	0	9	4	0	0	8	5	0	0	13	0	0	0
13) Raoul	2	7	3	1	2	8	2	1	3	7	2	1	3	6	3	1	6	5	2	0

ORGANIZATIONAL SELF-AWARENESS

Summarized Totals of the (Good + Poor) Categories

Name	Team Player	Relationship	Trust	Communication	Attitude	Total
1) Chin	3	2	3	2	2	12
2) Sherry	1	2	2	-	1	6
3) Sophia	9	10	10	4	9	42
4) Leroy	1	2	-	2	3	8
5) Juanita	6	6	10	8	10	40
6) Byron	-	1	3	1	2	7
7) Vladimir	6	7	9	7	2	31
8) Bessie	2	1	1	2	1	7
9) Mohammad	3	4	2	9	-	18
10) Daryl	1	-	1	1	-	3
11) Valerie	2	5	3	1	3	14
12) Karen	1	-	-	-	-	1
13) Raoul	4	3	3	4	2	16

Organizational Self-Awareness
(Totals of Good and Poor Categories)

Name	(G+P)
Karen	1
Daryl	3
Sherry	6
Byron	7
Bessie	7
Leroy	8
Chin	12
Valerie	14
Raoul	16
Mohammad	18
Vladimir	31
Juanita	40
Sophia	42

Results Interpretation

Each individual is given a form as shown on page 136. He or she circles one entry for each characteristic, including himself or herself. Selection for an entry is based upon one's experience and/or intuition of that person, where proof is unnecessary.

Page 138 is a tabulation of the entries for each characteristic for each of the 13 participants. This tabulation is the result of all 13 evaluations and is normally kept confidential. Someone other than the 13 participants usually performs this tabulation.

Page 139 is the sum of the Good (G) and Poor (P) entries for each characteristic for each participant. It is assumed that Good (G) and Poor (P) are ratings that require improvement. Obviously, the larger a number relating to a characteristic, the more it is perceived by the group that that characteristic is experienced as a difficulty with the person evaluated. When the numbers are relatively large, it is very difficult for a person to deny he or she has a problem.

Page 140 is the numerical total for each participant (last column on page 139). When distributed to the group, the names are omitted. However, it is clear that Vladimir, Juanita, and Sophia have definite interpersonal problems within the group structure. Others have specific difficulties: Mohammad has communication problems (page 139); Raoul could improve overall (page 139); Valerie might improve in the area of relationships (page 139).

Chapter Six

Wisdom—Your Soul Connection

"To gain a little every day is knowledge,
To lose a little every day is wisdom."

Lao-Tzu

Introduction

I suspect that when most of us think of the word *wisdom*, we tend to associate it with prophets, shamans, sages or, possibly, people of letters. However, as used in this book, *wisdom is an in-depth understanding, empathy, and compassion for the human experience.* It implies a knowing that goes beyond a system of values and judgments. Wisdom, in practice, is being intimately involved in everyday life and yet not ruled by its constraints when gently touched by a spiritual calling. As the focus on people continues to dominate the way work is performed, there will be greater necessity for an in-depth knowledge of those with whom we work. This chapter will show how wisdom plays a natural part in workplace functioning, in activities such as mentoring, teaming, personal empowerment, and the exploration of one's creative consciousness. As the workplace continues to be subjected to the stresses of accelerated change and continuous learning, wisdom will increasingly become a necessary adaptive skill.

What Is Wisdom?

Have you ever had the experience of unconditional acceptance by someone when you were at the worst point in your life—a point at which you perhaps experienced total humility or nonbeing? For example, during the prehistoric period of hunting and foraging, the ultimate sentence of a clan member was not death. That was an everyday occurrence. Instead, it was banishment—the collective agreement by the group of the nonexistence of a particular group member. This action is so devastating because it means the "unrelatedness" of a person with respect to the group. Since relatedness is *the* nature of the human experience, then banishment sets one adrift with no connectedness, orientation, or ground of being. On the other hand, to have someone available who unconditionally accepts you and acknowledges your *inherent* worth as a human being is a reflection of that person's in-depth understanding of what you are experiencing. The source of this way of being and behaving is spiritual.

Wisdom is a state of being that gives rise to spiritually-sourced behavior. Wisdom, in practice, deals more with the observation and acceptance of the human experience than it does with judgment and advice. One's acceptance of how another may choose to live their life establishes a relationship of trust between those individuals. And trust is the essential ingredient for having permission to assist another through their process of personal transformation. Wisdom also provides the insight for the most proactive way of facilitating the transformation process.

The following story of Jacqueline Bernstein illustrates how wisdom plays out in mentoring in a workplace where spirituality is validated.

Jacqueline Bernstein—Learning to Be Yourself

Jacqueline Bernstein worked for a large retail corporation in the Midwest. Her rise within the organization had been by way of the fast track because of her strong career focus. Jackie, as she was fondly called, was acknowledged as bright, energetic, and skilled at relating to people. Although she had held several jobs within the organization, she excelled in retail buying from the world market. Jackie was mentored by the vice president of marketing, Marilyn Scott, who had come up through the ranks when career women were not only unwelcome, but outright resented as well. Marilyn had succeeded in spite of such difficulties because of a long history of having practiced meditation based on Eastern philosophies. Marilyn's incorporation of these techniques was no secret to anyone and was often the source of light humor, which she secretly enjoyed. If humor was a way to legitimize her spiritual practices during the work day and at the same time make her colleagues comfortable with them, then it was a win/win situation for everyone.

During one of their mentoring dinners, Marilyn suggested to Jackie that she explore a personal development workshop that she, Marilyn, had taken some years ago. Marilyn cautioned Jackie that the workshop was quite in-depth and even confrontive at times. She indicated that she was recommending the workshop because she felt that as Jackie began to move into the upper ranks of leadership, Jackie's ability to maintain a sense of calmness and composure in trying situations would be closely monitored by her supervisors. Marilyn also indicated that this workshop, which had been her own initial entry point into personal development, involved practices that she still regularly used to keep her in touch with her spirituality. "In any case," Marilyn said, "give it some thought, because there are a million ways of accomplishing the same objective."

During the weeks that followed, Jackie became progressively more interested in Marilyn's idea of personal development. Jackie realized that she had increasingly begun to bring home the stress that related to comments by her fellow workers about her single marital status. She usually worked off such stressful feelings by way of a dedicated exercise program. However, Jackie found that she was gradually beginning to experience increased irritation and less tolerance for people's "amusing" comments in this regard. Moreover, some of the more recent comments had suggested that she might be a lesbian. Jackie was beginning to sense that others were picking up on her increasing irritation. As a result, she contacted Marilyn to inquire as to how she might get more information about the workshop.

After further discussion with Marilyn, Jackie decided to enroll in the week-long program. When she arrived at the retreat site in Vail, Colorado, Jackie discovered that she was there with twenty-five other participants, all from corporate America. As the week progressed, Jackie began to experience deeply held feelings and emotions that related to the way she had consciously avoided situations with men that might lead to marriage. By way of justification, she had always reasoned that her single status had allowed her to succeed at such a young age. By the end of the workshop, Jackie's elaborate justifications for remaining single, as a necessity for success, were all but shattered. In fact, what Jackie discovered, was that her avoidance of possible marital relationships actually stemmed from her early childhood experience of her parents' divorce. The underlying intent behind her resistance, she realized, was to keep herself from experiencing the same kind of painful separation that her mother had gone through.

When she returned to work the following week, Jackie immediately met with Marilyn to discuss her realization. She confided to her mentor that without the workshop, she would have had no idea of the degree to which she had suppressed these feelings over the years. Jackie had always believed that it was important to "look" happy and cheerful even if you felt horrible inside. It was now apparent to her that her habit of acting one way and feeling another was the source of increased stress and conflict in her life to such an extent that even exercising could not totally eliminate it. What had made the situation even worse was that there was no one outside of the workplace in whom she could really confide about her true feelings. Marilyn listened understandingly while Jackie continued to share for more than an hour. It was as if thirty-five years of bottled feelings and emotions were pouring out in a matter of minutes.

At the conclusion of Jackie's disclosure, Marilyn confided that she had begun to see the signs of increased stress in Jackie's face and body language. In fact, this had been the reason why Marilyn had suggested the workshop in the first place. Marilyn explained that she knew that sooner or later this internal conflict would show up in Jackie's work and possibly lead to an incident that might seriously jeopardize Jackie's career plans. Marilyn then suggested that Jackie consider exploring additional personal, and possibly spiritual, development materials and activities that Jackie would feel personally comfortable with. These materials and activities would help Jackie more fully understand her realization and continue the process of personal growth. Finally, Marilyn indicated that whether an individual is male or female, having some form of personal discipline for adapting to change was essential to functioning effectively, particularly when one is in a leadership role.

Jackie was fortunate to be a part of an organization that allowed (but did not require) spirituality in the workplace. She was also fortunate to have a mentor who recognized a situation that could have adversely affected her career. Marilyn's understanding of Jackie's situation led to the *suggestion* of the workshop Jackie attended and to her further developing a continuing process of self-improvement. In this situation, the ultimate measure of Jackie's transformation was her greater tolerance for the shortcomings of others when they made uncomplimentary comments about her. Jackie also developed an ability to be "centered" in stressful situations as a result of a dedicated commitment she developed to practicing Yoga. This pattern of centered being and behaving were the result of expanded wisdom. This means that Jackie can now mentor others who face similar situations as she did, just as Marilyn had mentored her. The essence of this story is that Jackie took advantage of the opportunity she was given to integrate personal and spiritual growth into her everyday work life; and it paid off for her in a very real way. The message: use workplace conflict as an opportunity for gaining greater wisdom about self and others as a powerful adaptive skill.

Personal Growth and Performance Go Hand-in-Glove

What is the relationship between in-depth personal exploration and workplace performance? Responses to this question are the theme of this section. As we discussed in the previous chapter, individuality is created by the unique way we structure our view of reality. When this view is integrated with our inbred survival instinct, we tend to believe that our way of thinking is not only right, but that it is also superior to others. This sense of superiority is called ethnocentrism. An extreme form of ethnocentrism is xenophobia—the fear of even experiencing differences.

Unless we consciously train our mind in self-awareness skills—in the same way we would work to acquire necessary technical skills—continual interpersonal conflict and incremental personal growth will be the result. Under these limiting conditions, the opportunity for breakthrough performance is effectively prevented because breakthroughs in personal growth are a necessary part of the process. The following story is an example of this relationship between personal growth and performance.

Getting Down to Business

During the early 1990s, Texas Instruments (TI) came to the conclusion that self-managed teams were necessary for maintaining a profitable operation. As a result, teamwork was comprehensively integrated into the TI culture. As a part of that integration process, the Corporate Services business unit was supported by a human resources group called the High-Performance Support Team. This effort was led by the Vice President of Corporate Environmental, Safety, and Health, Shaunna Sowell.

In this assignment, Shaunna played the role of lead facilitator in establishing self-managed teams in Corporate Services and other parts of the TI organization. Having embraced personal growth as a natural part of her own life, Shaunna's experience was that "change primarily occurs as a result of a significant emotional event." Therefore, whenever she encountered a conflict within herself or with others, Shaunna sought solutions that involved changing both people *and* processes. On the other hand, many of her colleagues resisted this dual approach to performance improvement, but instead attempted to solve problems by merely changing *processes* and *procedures*. When Shaunna suggested that personal growth might be an important part of a solution, her colleagues often felt confronted.

One of the organizations that Shaunna facilitated was charged with supporting the operations of an advanced semiconductor manufacturing plant. The organization was comprised of fifteen engineers and technicians and twenty-five skilled mechanics. It was operated by the traditional management style of command and control. The plant manager, who was their primary customer, was extremely dissatisfied with the quality, cost, and cycle time of the service he had been receiving from the support organization. He believed that the people in the organization were simply not capable of meeting his expectations.

In assessing the department's operation, Shaunna came to the following conclusions: the people in the organization did not understand their customer's needs;

and they believed they had little power to make changes in how their work was done. These same people, outside of the workplace, were heads of households, community leaders, coaches, church leaders, and even owned small businesses on the side. Yet within the workplace, they simply followed directions.

Shaunna determined that in order for them to be successful, the organization's work processes would have to be redesigned so that the performance capacity of everyone involved could be fully utilized. It is important to mention that Shaunna's personal philosophy is that people want to excel. If they do not, she believes, it is either because barriers exist in the system or within people themselves that need to be removed. It is the role of leadership, Shaunna believed, to establish processes that remove such barriers and facilitate people in achieving the level of excellence of which they are capable.

Under Shaunna's leadership, the organization began by reassessing their customer's expectations and establishing baselines on their current level of performance. Then they established improvement processes and goals, dismantled the hierarchy within the organization, organized small work teams, and created accountability systems. Within eighteen months, the department had reduced the cost of their services by 100%, reduced cycle time by 300%, and improved quality by 100%. Their once-dissatisfied customer now considered them a quality supplier and the level of job satisfaction, within the department itself, improved 30%.

All this was accomplished by the same people who had previously been considered poor suppliers and even failures by their primary customer and management. The primary problem was a lack of leadership support that was necessary for them to perform to their full capacity. Once Shaunna began facilitating the process, employees also began to discover their own internal barriers to performance. These personal barriers were primarily related to owning a greater sense of personal responsibility and accountability for their performance— a genuine ownership of the results they were creating. As these issues were resolved, the job of creating and mastering new processes and procedures was relatively easily accomplished.

The overriding motivation of the people in the organization was to be successful, in spite of the sometimes painful process of personal growth they experienced. The key element in their success was the leadership of someone who cared and believed in their ability to achieve excellence.

Wisdom and Personal Empowerment

In Chapter Three, we defined personal empowerment as an individual's capacity to perform—where performance is measured in terms of meeting or preferably exceeding the expectations of customers. We also noted that different individuals have different potentials for performing. In order to achieve high performance, it is necessary for each of us to move beyond self-limiting beliefs we may have about ourselves, the people we work with, and our workplace. In other words, what we presently believe can be a limitation in exploring the depths of our potential.

For example, if you are a scientist or an engineer and are *attached* to the belief that science is the study of reality, then that belief might be a limitation in terms of creating the next paradigm of scientific exploration. In the next paradigm, we may discover that science is only indirectly related to reality—that what science actually does is *mimic* reality. In contemplating these assertions, we might consider the statement of Werner Heisenberg, one of the creators of quantum mechanics:

> *"What we observe is not nature itself,*
> *but nature exposed to our*
> *method of questioning."*

As we begin to push the limits of human capacity, we must dismantle existing paradigms that restrict our thinking. The courage to push beyond such limitations is the prerequisite for exploring expanded levels of consciousness. Through this process we can learn to become creative, innovative, and imaginative on demand.

Identifying and creating paradigms requires greater wisdom. The extent to which we are willing to explore beyond our well-founded systems of belief is directly proportional to how personally empowered we can become in terms of performance. When Muhammed Ali (then known as Cassius Clay) declared that he would defeat Sonny Liston (the reigning heavyweight boxing champion), he had moved beyond the paradigm of "the invincibility of Liston" which was believed by most sports writers. *Their* beliefs did not matter nor control the mind-set of Ali. As a result, the existing paradigm of Liston's invincibility was shattered when Ali defeated Liston. Thus, it is important to recognize that when you experience a sense of "intuitive surety," you are probably tapping into your inner wisdom. A whole new dimension of who you are and what you are capable of spontaneously appears when you learn to trust this internal prompting.

Several years ago, a very good friend who is 80% American-Native, was struggling with an inner conflict. She had become successful as the administrator of a state-wide human services program. Her struggle resulted from an inner prompting that she wanted to do something else professionally. While her administrative job no longer held any passion for her, she and her family had developed a high standard of living based on her salary. Choosing between family and self became her core dilemma. She felt stuck at this point, particularly since she had chosen not to share her dilemma with her husband.

Her internal conflict was further exacerbated by the fact that American-Native practices involving "truth telling" had been part of her life since she was 5 years old. As a result of confronting her dilemma, she experienced several months of intense emotional cleansing and was able to move from the paradigm of "self *or* others" to "self *and* others." The culmination of this process was her realization that she wanted to teach and counsel at a small community college. Being at peace with her realization, my friend simply informed her family of her decision to change jobs and career. Perhaps not surprisingly, her family understood and accepted the finality of her decision, and they all got on with their lives.

Oddly enough, the only real protest she experienced came from her supervisor at the human services organization. He simply could not understand her decision to change careers. He asked her, "Why are you doing this? What are you thinking? Why would you ever make such a decision?" My friend simply replied, "Because it pleases me to do so. It makes me happy."

Aligning the wisdom of your life purpose with your natural and learned competencies drives empowered, passionate participation in life. An essential requirement for this level of participation is the continual acquisition of new knowledge and skills.

You Have to Know Something to Produce Something

While personal exploration is necessary, exploration alone is not sufficient to produce a product or service that is a quantum jump beyond what already exists. The ability to *manifest* a creative idea significantly beyond that which is already known is based upon one's in-depth knowledge of a relevant field or subject. Children experience the same creative process as adults do. Their ability to put their ideas into some form, however, is limited by their skills and what they know. Hence, their inventions, crafts, and paintings become more sophisticated as their learning progresses. Einstein had an in-depth knowledge of mathematics and physics as a necessity for creating the Theory of Relativity. His breakthrough in physics also resulted in an expanded understanding of the human experience, which we have defined in this chapter as wisdom. The following statement by Einstein *is a result* of his in-depth creative exploration:

> *A human being is part of the whole, called by us the "Universe," a part limited in time and space. He experiences himself, his thoughts,*

and feelings as something separated from the rest—a kind of optical delusion of his consciousness. This delusion is a kind of prison for us, restricting us to our personal desires and to affection for a few persons nearest to us. Our task must be to free ourselves from this prison by widening our circle of compassion to embrace all living creatures and the whole of nature in its beauty.

Wisdom is the result of expanded personal empowerment, and is unlimited in capacity. Therefore, living up to your full capability requires:

1) A dedicated process of *self-motivated* continuous learning—acquiring new knowledge and skills.

2) The continuous development of your creative ability as a part of your everyday life.

3) A dedicated program of personal and spiritual growth.

4) The wisdom to discover your life's purpose and the courage to live it.

Your Spiritual Self Is Really Running Things

It is not unusual for those on a path of personal growth to find themselves suddenly faced with a major change. Such a change commonly occurs to individuals who have created a connection or a channel to their inner wisdom. It is also not unusual, when an inner prompting occurs, for such individuals to experience conflict with their present life situation. The spiritually driven force for self-expression is so powerful that it is practically unstoppable, no matter what the "real world" consequences might be. Those consequences might include such things as a change in marital status, work activity, family responsibilities, or discovering and living your life purpose. In other words, your spiritual self "sees" things from a greater perspective than your human self. It is ultimately in control of the choices you make. Individuals who "know in their hearts" what they must do have always been faced with this dichotomy. From a spiritual perspective, there is no dichotomy. The dichotomy is transcended. This type of classic dilemma is illustrated by the story of Lydia and Barry.

Barry created a small business dealing with organizational development. He had recently resigned from a secure and successful position he had held for twenty years with a major corporation. The products and services of the new company were the result of Barry's creativity in personal and organizational transformation. Lydia joined Barry as a part-time associate in the early stages of the business' growth, and then as a full-time employee a year later. Lydia and Barry enjoyed working together and they both embraced the process of challenging personal growth as a regular part of their lives. As a result of their joint commitment, the business prospered beyond their wildest dreams. Their close personal relationship also led to their getting married and having two children together.

At deeper personal levels, Barry and Lydia were both growing and changing at a tremendous pace as a result of their in-depth spiritual exploration. What neither of them consciously recognized, however, was that their spiritual paths were becoming unaligned in regard to operating and developing the business. As a result, they held conflicting views with respect to the following questions: "How do we best operate the business?" "In what direction should the business grow?" and "Who should make final decisions?" Conflict—inner and outer—is the natural result of change. If conflict is not constructively addressed and accommodated, it persists. Intense persistent conflict is a harbinger of major change that ultimately aligns a person with their spiritual agenda—whether they are consciously aware of that agenda or not.

Lydia finally decided to leave the business and create her own organization. Lydia and Barry's personal conflict ultimately led to separation and finally to divorce. Lydia appears to have found happiness with her own business and has a clear sense of her spiritually driven calling. Barry has likewise continued to run a successful business.

The point of this story is that once a spiritual connection is made, such as Lydia experienced, it is practically impossible to ignore it or shut it down. From a human perspective, the challenge for us is in learning how to be *comfortable* with dichotomy. On one hand is satisfying one's *self*, and on the other, there is the seemingly opposite commitment to *others*. One's human actions will appear to favor one or the other, depending on who is making the observation and interpretation. But one's spiritual self views this seeming dichotomy as one, since satisfying self and others is inseparable—irrespective of the resulting life situation. In the case of Lydia and Barry, remaining together, separating, and divorcing are all acceptable to one's spiritual self. We are loved and accepted by our spiritual self regardless of the life choices we make. Ultimately, being *aligned* and *integrated* physically, mentally, and spiritually as a person, is the *only* sustainable source of certainty in decision making. That sense of certainty comes from within. That is wisdom.

Wisdom Is All Around and within Us

Actually, wisdom is not anything new to the workplace. It simply has not been acknowledged and legitimized as essential to organizational success—at least not in the Western world. Wisdom has always been valued and integral to the way non-Western organizations and societies have functioned. The business traditions of Japan are firmly rooted in the principles of Buddha (Buddhism) and Sun-Tzu (The Art of War) and those of China in Lao-Tzu (Taoism) and Confucius. There is wisdom in the familiar saying that "We must learn equally from the wisdom of others, since we individually don't make enough mistakes of our own to learn how much we need to know." When we learn something new, it is commonly because something we previously believed is no longer valid. Being open to continually changing our reality is the key to acquiring wisdom.

Reflecting on the quote at the beginning of this chapter by Lao-Tzu,

"To gain a little every day is knowledge,
To lose a little every day is wisdom,"

his words would appear at first to be paradoxical. However, if we recall that our definition of wisdom is: understanding, empathy, and compassion for the human experience; then losing a little everyday means regularly releasing an opinion, idea, belief, or value about how life should be. What is important here is that a belief which is released does not have to be replaced with a different one. What replaces it is a "natural way of being." This is why we describe wisdom as a way of being. A natural way of being occurs when we let go of our assumptions of "how it should be," "how it could be," and "how it ought to be," and just accept "how it is," as a *prelude* to interacting with others. This is the continual process of losing a little every day.

A Personal Flashback

In 1978 I began a dedicated process of personal growth. This process originated from my experience of working with my Euro-American colleagues as Chairman of the Chemistry Department at the University of Utah. It was then that I began to learn of the biases and prejudices *I* had adopted while growing up in New Orleans, Louisiana. I soon relearned what it meant to be personally responsible, but in a racial context where I had formerly believed I had been victimized. Taking responsibility for my own contribution to interpersonal dysfunction in the area of race was a significant breakthrough in my own personal development. It provided the basis for the confidence I acquired in competing on an uneven playing field without feeling victimized.

These breakthroughs were so significant in reshaping my life in positive ways that I began exploring philosophies and disciplines from other parts of the world, namely China, Japan, South America, and Europe. To my surprise, much of what I learned significantly enhanced my research activities at the university. Those activities involved devising elaborate research experiments, figuring out scientific puzzles, and creating explanations for the experimental observations we obtained. The personal discipline practices I learned to utilize included creative visualization, sleep-state and subliminal programming, closed-eye exercises, meditation, and quantum-thinking.

Since a crucial part of performing basic research is being able to operate *beyond* the present limits of one's creative ability, this requirement led me to the deeper exploration of consciousness. These explorations involved paradigm identification (quantum-thinking), paradigm creation, and experiencing the deepest levels of consciousness in terms of expanded human potential. It was during this process in 1985 that I experienced the creation of a channel to my creative consciousness. Although this channel provided a constant source of new information and ideas for scientific research, it also spontaneously transmitted information that was contrary to some of the most fundamental beliefs that I considered to be reality. For example, one message included the axiom: "There is no objective reality. Reality is a function of humankind's rich imagination." Transmissions of this nature prompted me to rethink the wisdom of my in-depth explorations. Eventually, one of Picasso's statements (which was quoted earlier in this book) began to explain the source of my discomfort and confusion:

> *"The act of creation is simultaneously
> the act of destruction."*

The greater the depth of exploration, the greater the challenge to our present beliefs about reality, since our beliefs about reality continually change as we acquire greater wisdom. In this case, my state of discomfort and confusion persisted for about six months. Then one day "out of the blue," this skinny, bearded guy who owned a metaphysical bookstore stormed into my life. We began an innocent conversation about a recently written book on consciousness. As our conversation proceeded, I got the uneasy feeling that he was really asking me questions to discover how open I was to metaphysical ideas. I was not only open, but desperate for someone to explain all that had been happening to me. Through a series of discussions, I began to better understand those dimensions of consciousness that are not subject to the "laws" of the Cartesian-Newtonian paradigm. This understanding provided me an expanded view of my research activities and greater detachment from their underlying assumptions. Detachment is the key element for unlimited exploration of one's creative consciousness and a greater mastery of the events occurring in one's life. For me, the skinny, bearded guy was definitely an example of the saying, "When the student is ready, the teacher will appear."

Conclusion

So where are we? Wisdom is a way of being that is the natural result of personal and spiritual transformation. It is an in-depth understanding, empathy, and compassion for the human experience. As the workplace becomes increasingly diverse from human, cultural, and systems perspectives, it is clear that resolutions beyond ordinary problem-solving or compromise will be necessary for successful business functioning. Therefore, everyone in the work force will need to master this "skill of being" in proportion to his or her level of responsibility.

This conclusion was perhaps best captured by Albert Einstein, who said:

> *"The world that we have made as a result*
> *of the level of thinking we have done*
> *thus far, creates problems that we cannot*
> *solve at the level we have created them."*

The problems to which he refers, can only be solved through expanded personal and collective wisdom, and perhaps, a new paradigm for human existence. This new paradigm will be disussed in Chapter Eight. In order to operate in this new paradigm, we require an expanded definition of leadership, which is the subject of the following chapter.

Listed on the following pages are suggestions of how to incorporate wisdom into your everyday interactions with others—both in the workplace and in your personal life.

Nuggets of Wisdom*

The following are practical behaviors that you might incorporate into your work life, where appropriate:

1. *Demonstrate more confidence in others.*

   - Allow others to create (and follow) their own solutions even when you suspect they are wrong.
   - Express your support of their decisions and actions.
   - Require less approval of their actions.
   - Don't question the motives of others.
   - Don't ignore the input of other people.

2. *Have patience with others.*

   - Give others time to come up with their own solutions.
   - Don't interrupt or finish other people's sentences for them.
   - Withhold making premature judgments on the abilities and commitment of others.

3. *Creating turmoil might win the battle, but lose the war.*

   - Deal with everybody on a peer-to-peer level at all times.
   - Don't inject emotionally charged language into a situation.
   - Rely on intuition *and* reason, rather than intimidation, to sway others.

*Source: Thomas Cannon, Ph.D.

4. *You have ultimate control out of a total absence of control.*

- Describe rather than prescribe.
- Let others establish the agenda, constraints, and timetables for work affecting them.
- Illuminate visions.
- Identify interrelationships between actions and consequences and let others decide on actions to take.

5. *You can't create closeness with intimidation.*

- Set aside rank in dealing with subordinates.
- Listen to others holding different views.
- Don't flaunt degrees and credentials.
- Support the self-esteem of others by expressing confidence in their abilities and applauding their efforts.

6. *Treat every interaction as if it were crucial to success.*

- Place an imaginary video camera in the room.
- Treat every individual like you would treat the president of the company.
- Stay plugged into every conversation, no matter how minor.

7. *Assume every case is that one of ten cases when you're wrong.*

- Admit the possibility of being wrong.
- Actively solicit alternative ideas.
- Really listen to other suggestions and find a way to try them out.

8. ***Positive results must always include the impact on people.***

   - Stay in tune with how your behavior is affecting others.
   - Consider how you would feel if you were placed in the other person's situation.
   - Think of how you will view this episode when you are 90 years old.
   - Value other people's views and suggestions.

9. ***Worth and value are inherent and independent of achievements.***

   - Frequently step back and take the view from 10,000 light years away.
   - Remember your oneness with all other entities within the universe.
   - Quit keeping score.

Chapter Seven

The New Leadership— Spirituality

"True leaders inspire people to do great things and when the work is done, their people proudly say, We did this ourselves."

Lao-Tzu

Introduction

The requirements for being in business changed dramatically over the last fifteen years of the 20th Century. This phenomenon paralleled the onset of the Knowledge-based Age, which began about 1985. Within this paradigm, the ability to create new knowledge was the essential element in developing new products and services. Information, capital, and land were less limiting than in previous paradigms. This shift allowed countries we have traditionally described as "underdeveloped" and "developing" to play significant roles in the global business community. These include India, Pakistan, and Pacific Rim countries such as Thailand, South Korea, Singapore, Hong Kong, and the Philippines; and China stands poised to play a dominant role in the 21st Century. As a result of this expanded participation in mainstream business, the requirements of leadership have also expanded.

Leadership is the ability to influence the thinking, commitment, and behaviors of others. Leading begins with a vision that is compelling as compared to a presently existing state. Leadership in action involves enrolling others in the process of achieving that vision. It is concluded when the vision becomes reality. In Chapter Five, we discussed the vision of Tim Berners-Lee to have the global Internet become a reality. His vision was "to make a world of information readily available to everyone." It took Berners-Lee nine years to fully develop that vision. During this period he stated, "Keeping your vision an unstated 'gut feeling' for as long as possible is rather important. The moment you write down your vision, you limit the directions and possibilities your mind can come up with. You stop the subconscious creative process which allows your ideas to mature as a tangle of random, half-known associations." Once his vision was crystallized, he focused on bringing the World Wide Web to life. It took four years to persuade the various seed communities that it was a good idea. In 1991, the Internet became a reality.

In this chapter, we will explore the subject of leadership as it relates to today's rapidly changing business environment. Much of the discussion will involve leadership in the midst of change—both internal and external. We will explore the subjects of self-knowledge, vision, and leadership in action. The chapter concludes with a discussion of the requirements of the New Leadership resulting from the emergence of the Age of Spirituality.

The First Step—Know Thyself

Leadership begins with a knowledge of self. The phrase "know thyself" is the ancient Delphic inscription from Thebes in Greece. It refers to the continuing process of in-depth self-exploration beyond the limitations of personal consciousness. It means communication with one's soul. Communication with this inner source provides clarity as to one's life purpose. Aligning your life purpose with your natural talents, skills, and abilities is the first step to spiritual leadership. This natural inner drive to self-express is the source of commitment and passion.

Well-known historical spiritual leaders include Dr. Martin Luther King Jr., Mohandas K. Gandhi, and Chief Joseph. This classification becomes more confusing, or even controversial, when we consider individuals such as Malcolm X, Anwar Sadat, Yitzhak Shamir, Abraham Lincoln, or Susan B. Anthony. Nevertheless, each of these individuals went through the deeply personal process of self-understanding as a prelude to the leadership roles they played in life. In a like manner, I believe the present workplace is abundant with spiritual leaders. They are dispersed throughout large and small organizations. Many of them have simply not publicly declared their spirituality for personal reasons.

They are the teachers who influenced your formative years; the physician who lovingly tended you back to health physically, mentally, and spiritually; the CEO who took a stand for equal opportunity irrespective of the business consequences; the boss who supported your personal and professional growth; the co-worker who was always there in difficult times; and the employee who lives spiritual values as a way of life. They are the vanguard for the transformation that will acknowledge and validate spirituality as a functional business necessity in the workplace. The following story describes how Janice Hoffman significantly expanded her business mission as a result of learning quantum-thinking.

Janice Hoffman—Exploring the Depths of Self

Janice Hoffman is president of an entertainment business that is located in southern California. She produces, directs, and writes for television. She is extremely creative in all aspects of entertainment. For more than ten years she has been on a dedicated path of personal and spiritual growth. Janice is aware that her business success depends on her ability to access the deepest levels of her creative consciousness.

Several years ago, Janice began the process of learning quantum-thinking. This challenging process propelled her into a degree of personal exploration that she had never previously experienced. Since Janice's background is important in understanding her personal exploration, it is important to know that she was reared in a very religious family. Her parents believed in strict rules of how children should be raised. Overall, her childhood family life was very structured. In her teenage years, Janice constantly got into trouble, possibly as a way of rebelling against her structured childhood. What she did not realize at the time, however, was that being "bad" was simply the opposite side of the dichotomy of being "good." As a result, her internal struggle involving the concepts of "good" and "bad" behaviors would dominate her life until she could gain the wisdom to transcend them both. This insight into one's self is accomplished by first, the deeply introspective process of acknowledging that one's own fabricated beliefs are the source of conflict in one's life and not the expectations of one's parents. Second, the acceptance of total responsibility for the results created by one's behaviors—irrespective of whether the results are classified as good or bad. One then no longer strives to be "good," driven by a concept of "good behavior," but is finally free to live life naturally. Let's observe how this two-step process played out in Janice's success in achieving quantum-thinking.

During the process of creative exploration, Janice discovered deeply hidden barriers to her creative ability that related to her childhood upbringing. These barriers involved strongly held beliefs about her worth or value as a person based upon her religious upbringing. Janice also discovered that value, worth, and structured behavior were all related in her reality. They were the basis upon which she evaluated herself as a good or bad person. Her breakthrough was the realization that her fundamental belief about herself was not valid: "I am worthy if I am good." After several weeks of internalizing the falsity of this statement, Janice concluded that her value or worth as a person was independent of her behavior or accomplishments. *She was worthy by virtue of the fact that she was a human expression of spiritual consciousness.* Furthermore, no deed or accomplishment could make her more or less worthy. "Worth is a birthright!" Janice realized. She simply needed to recapture her sense of innate worth as a given, without the necessity of proof.

Janice also realized that "good behavior" meant attempting to live up to the expectations of others. And "bad behavior" was her attempt to be herself. This realization led her to accepting responsiblity for the role she played in creating continual conflict in her life. Discovering and transcending barriers at this level frees one to experience quantum-thinking. Therefore, the freedom to create, at the deepest level of your creative consciousness, requires the invalidation of a fundamental belief you may have about yourself that has no validity in experiential reality. This fundamental belief, by nature, is self-limiting.

As previously mentioned, spiritual growth of this nature also results in an expanded knowledge of self, which we have referred to as wisdom. This ability to discover yourself and in turn re-create your professional activities is sourced from wisdom. In Janice's case, her company re-created its mission, and expanded its entertainment activities into the areas of spiritual, metaphysical, and humanistic-oriented projects. Given this degree of clarity about one's self, it is possible to project a future state of activity that is naturally driven by passion and commitment. This ability is called visionary and the projected future state is called vision.

Vision

Having achieved clarity of self, one is now in a position to create (or re-create) the future. Creating the future is accomplished by establishing a vision. A lighthouse is my symbol of a vision. It is continually flashing in the distance to provide direction if we get off course. It stands tall, day and night, so that we can constantly remind ourselves of what it is we are attempting to accomplish. It also warns us of dangers we might experience that could threaten our success. Remember, the purpose of a lighthouse is to warn of shallow water or rocks that may threaten a ship's voyage. The story of Chris Harding illustrates how a spiritually sourced vision creates such inner turmoil that it will not be denied.

Chris Harding—The Fire Inside

Chris Harding, like Janice in the previous section, has been in the entertainment business for more than twenty years. Several years ago, he started experiencing a sense of discontentment in his work. He had done exceptional work in producing Disney television specials and movies such as "The Christmas Box" for CBS Television. On the set of The Christmas Box production, however, he noticed that his activity was primarily devoted to coaching others and systematically taking himself out of the picture. As the production proceeded, a question popped into his mind, "What am *I* doing here?" In moments of relaxation or inattention, this can either be an exciting or dangerous question, depending upon how we embrace personal change.

Chris was propelled into acknowledging that he wanted to do something different. He describes it as "a fire inside of me." Obviously, the fire had been there for some time, probably on slow burn. He describes the process as coming to the end of an era in his life. He was now free to consciously explore questions like, "What is it *I* want to do?" and "What am *I* naturally drawn to?" As he asked himself these questions, he began writing thoughts that popped into his mind. His initial thoughts comprised ten pages of written ideas. The general theme that kept running through these written notes was "to create an atmosphere for the highest likelihood for people to succeed." The shift occurring within him also involved moving from "hands-on" to "overseeing." These ideas soon became the founding pieces of a vision for a company he wanted to create.

What I have not mentioned is that personal and spiritual growth are an integrated part of Chris's life. As a result, he has learned how to *observe* others and himself in the process of living. He views life more as a continual workshop of self-discovery than a process of achieving goals. He views goals as milestones to set this "life workshop" into motion. Several years ago, Chris began the serious practice of Zen. This practice involves meditation, koan studies, and one-on-one interviews with the sensei (or Zen leader). A koan is a riddle without a solution used to provoke sudden enlightenment, e.g., "What is the sound of one hand clapping?" The practice of Zen was central in Chris's moving through this transition in his life without the necessity of a crisis. Many of us move through major transitions by creating crises such as a major confrontation at work, illness, or poor performance so that someone else can be responsible for our transition. None of these crises were necessary in Chris's situation.

When Chris decided to take action regarding a career change, his ten pages of notes immediately became a clearly defined vision: "Acquire, develop, produce, and distribute entertainment products that have a transformational or spiritual spin." Before informing his present employer about his decision, he had a discussion with his family about his intention to change careers. He informed them that they should be prepared in the event his decision might lead to leaving the company and possible difficult times that might follow.

Before Chris had an opportunity to inform his employer of his decision, a vice president approached him and asked, "Chris, what would you do if you had the opportunity to start a spin-off company?" As Chris shared his vision, his vice president confided he had a similar vision. Chris, the vice president, and other key colleagues prepared a written proposal of how their vision could be aligned with the corporation's goals and mission. After receiving the proposal, the executive leadership of the company considered it for two months. During this period, Chris shares that he was totally detached from their decision. His detachment was based on an "inner knowing" that by pursuing his vision, he was doing the right thing for himself. He felt assured that his next professional activity would be forthcoming, whether or not the proposal was accepted. Then, to Chris's surprise, the company decided to invest in the idea.

As the start-up began, Chris had very definite ideas about the nature of the products, the management system, and the relationship of the employees to the products. Like the automobile manufacturer, Saturn, he wanted to create "a different kind of company." The entertainment products he had in mind would be family oriented. They would involve values relating to responsibility, empowerment, leadership, compassion, equality, hope, faith, and love—all spiritually derived concepts. The philosophy of the newly formed company would be that all team members become living examples of the products the company distributed. The employees and the products would be one.

Within several years of creating the new company, Chris's team had delivered over a dozen highly rated movies to the networks, established a growing home video company, and pushed some of the company's records to

#1 on the New Age radio charts. In spite of his success, a growing level of conflict existed between Chris and the parent corporation. This situation forced Chris to come to the challenging realization that his vision was not totally aligned with the vision of the parent corporation. As a result, he made the decision to leave the company in order to allow both himself and the parent corporation the opportunity to be true to their respective visions and dreams.

Chris was able to reach an amicable parting agreement with the parent corporation. He is now in the process of setting up an independent company that will allow him to pursue his vision without the restrictions and concerns that were inherent in the previous situation. Though many have expressed how illogical it is for him to pursue his dream at the expense of his job, Chris feels that the realization of his vision takes priority over the seeming sense of security that a job may bring.

The Learning—There are several leadership principles we might learn from Chris's experience:

1) Having in-depth knowledge of one's self is necessary for creating a vision that is compelling *and* lasting to both self and others.

2) Spiritual or personal growth practices can be crucial in making major life transitions without a crisis; and without creating victims or enemies.

3) One's level of risk-taking is in direct proportion to one's inner sense of security.

4)　The degree of fear experienced in making a major transition is significantly minimized if one has an in-depth understanding of himself or herself.

5)　Those involved in personal development achieve business objectives as effectively as those who are not, and they also preserve the well-being of self and others in the process.

As illustrated here, once a compelling vision is established, the next leadership challenge is transforming it into reality.

Leadership in Action

Leadership is tested most during periods of greatest challenge—or even crisis. External competition is rarely the greatest challenge. The greatest challenge is how we respond to the necessity for change. We either respond resistantly out of fear or proactively with determination—or a combination of both. Laura Henderson's process of redefining her business is an example of leadership in action.

Laura Henderson owns a modest-sized printing company in Phoenix, Arizona, that has prospered for more than fifteen years. Much of her success is due to her knowledge of advances in the business world—particularly those involving cost, quality, time, and consistently dependable service. With these elements in mind, she proposed to her staff that they invest in DocuTech equipment. She informed them that computer-based equipment would allow significant advances in production time, quality, and service. But most of all, she felt that if they did not invest in this new technology, their business could be seriously jeopardized by competitors.

Laura presented the proposal to her staff when business was exceptionally good. There were no major competitors using DocuTech. In fact, using the equipment at that time involved dealing with more maintenance problems than was cost-effective. Laura's staff primarily consisted of employees who had been with her from the start of the business. They were loyal and dedicated, but resistant to major changes. The greatest objection expressed by the staff was that they would need to learn about computers and the supporting technology. Some employees would also have to be retrained to become expert in various software programs and long-distance document transfers using modems. In addition, their present checks and balances which used dedicated personnel would have to be eliminated. As a result, everyone would have to operate in a more empowered manner to ensure the quality of their work. The more the staff realized the complete change this operation would bring, the more their resistance solidified, particularly since there *appeared* to be no immediate need for such a change from their perspective.

Laura decided that she would try a different approach in convincing her staff by describing a compelling future of expanded opportunity and greater prosperity. She also presented them with convincing business projections of how information technology would revolutionize business. She shared with her staff that she realized what a traumatic change this would be for many of them, but promised her unconditional support during the process. She also showed how the business objectives would eventually provide success that they could not now imagine, but that it involved risk-taking. The employees listened patiently, showed little enthusiasm, and proceeded to operate business as usual.

Laura was faced with a personal and professional dilemma. If she proceeded in spite of objections, she would lose many of her long-term loyal employees whom she had grown to love along with their families. If she did not proceed, she felt she would eventually lose the business, which provided significant meaning in her own life. Laura was faced with the "real-life" decision—self or others. At least this is how it appeared to her at the time (as opposed to self *and* others). In spite of the resistance from the majority, a few employees shared Laura's vision. They informed her that they would be there no matter what the outcome. One employee emerged with such dedication and commitment that Laura began a concerted process of mentoring her for a leadership role.

Laura proceeded to buy the DocuTech equipment with a loan secured by her home. When the equipment arrived, the new reality began to set in. Passive resistance changed to gossip and morale became a serious problem. Quality breakdowns as well as delayed shipments began to occur. At times Laura seriously wondered if she had made the wrong decision. Was all of this worth it for the sake of the business? At these times, those few who were committed to her vision would step in and provide leadership as well as encouragement. Laura came to realize that she probably would not have prevailed without their support. Such encouragement allowed her the opportunity to regain her bearings and focus on the job at hand. Long-term employees began leaving when it became clear that Laura was indeed going ahead with transforming the organization. During this transition, there were periods when things seemed to be stalled and Laura felt at a loss as to how to get things going again. In times such as these, she knew where she could find the inspiration she needed to get the process moving again. It involved getting away from the business, reconnecting spiritually, and returning with renewed commitment.

At the height of her crisis, Laura dropped everything and went off to an oceanside condominium for a week. She had often used this condominium retreat as a source of spiritual renewal. It was there, in fact, that she had gotten the idea for the new vision of her business. Contrary to her usual habit, Laura did not bring business papers or magazines with her and had no planned schedule. She was out of contact with the business during the entire week. Laura has always claimed that magical things happen to her at her private retreat. This crisis certainly required magic. Walking on the beach at night, Laura attempted to be receptive to her inner voice regarding what course of action she should take. Sometime during the latter part of the week, she got the flash of clarity she had been looking for and what actions she needed to take. She returned to Phoenix the next day with renewed conviction.

Laura called a staff meeting the Monday following her return and announced that she had decided to aggressively take the business into the future, regardless of the resistance that existed. She stated that everyone would have a week to decide if the new direction was best for them and their families. Although she wanted everyone to remain, she understood that this decision would force each person to reexamine their lives and their future plans. She announced that she would immediately be hiring two or three computer scientists to initiate the process as quickly as possible. In addition, the marketing and sales staff would have to be retrained to understand the new technology and how to sell it. What she wanted to make clear was that the organization was 100% committed to grow in the direction of information technology.

After the week of decision making, about one half of the old staff decided to find new opportunities. They indicated that things were moving too fast for them. One trusted employee confided to Laura that most of those leaving doubted the company would survive. As the doubtful employees left one by one, a new enthusiasm began to emerge in the organization. Those who stayed, along with new employees, began to re-create the organization. It is amazing how much momentum can be generated when an organization is left with those who are aligned with a single-minded purpose. In making the gradual transition over the next year and a half, the business struggled. The sales staff was faced with not only learning new technology, but also with creating an entirely new customer base. As of January 1999, however, the company is on a growth spiral that is leading to unprecedented success.

This example illustrates leadership in action—the proactive process of leading change in anticipation of the future business environment. The most decisive action occurs when a commitment is made to move forward in spite of the possible consequences.

The Learning—What we learn from this example are the following leadership characteristics:

1. *Vision* — The ability to *re-create* the vision of an organization in anticipation of the changing business environment.

2. *Risk-Taking* — The willingness to *live* the vision despite the possible loss of something considered to be highly valuable.

3. *Courage* — The willingness to *persevere* despite the fears associated with moving the organization into the future.

4. *Inspiration* — The ability to *communicate* with such emotion and dedication that others enthusiastically enroll in achieving the vision.

5. *Trust* — The ability to be sufficiently *believable*, both in personal and professional credibility, that others commit their futures with confidence.

6. *Persistence* — The willingness to *persevere* in spite of resistance, objections, and the time and energy necessary to progressively lead the organization in achieving the vision.

Getting Clear about Commitment

The three stages involved in the leadership process are:

Stage One: Creating a compelling vision of the future.

Stage Two: Enrolling, aligning, and facilitating others toward the achievement of the vision.

Stage Three: Achieving established goals and objectives defined by the vision.

The greatest challenge of leadership occurs in Stage Two as illustrated by the previous story of Laura Henderson. Progressively moving the process towards the manifestation of the vision involves resolving resistance, facilitating the transformation of others, and creatively responding to possible customer objections. Perhaps the greatest test in this process is self-commitment. That is, there will always be a point in the process where the leader faces the ultimate challenge in the form of a question: "Am *I* committed to this vision, as a majority of one, if being unsuccessful means possibly losing something I value highly?" "Value highly" may be one's home, savings, reputation, credit rating, credibility, position, status, or business.

A "yes" answer is a spiritual commitment. This means that the individual making the commitment has transcended the attachment to self-image or possessions that are considered to be highly valued. He or she has realized the distinction between personal (ego) attachments and the inherent value of self. Committing to the end in the pursuit of a vision in no way involves the value of self, regardless of the outcome. From this perspective, human value is not based upon image or achievements. It is based on the realization of self as a spiritual being having a human experience. Therefore, *human value is inherent*, not earned. Facilitating Stage Two has become more challenging as we have transitioned from the Knowledge-based to the Spiritual paradigm. This transition requires the mastery of new leadership skills to *complement* those from previous paradigms. The integration of these leadership characteristics is defined as the New Leadership.

The New Leadership

The New Leadership is a synthesis of:

Visionary leadership—which is vision-driven

Transformative leadership—which is learning-driven

Spiritual leadership—which is values-driven

Each of these characteristics will be discussed, in turn, below.

Visionary leadership is the ability to enroll others in achieving an accurate vision of the future. The vision needs to be sufficiently compelling so that others are self-enrolled to be a part of the process. Accurate visions are usually sourced from a spiritual connection. When Lee Iacocca was appointed President and CEO of the Chrysler Corporation in 1978, he had to secure a federal government loan to keep the company in business. His long-term vision was "to make Chrysler a global company." Douglas Fraser, President of the United Auto Workers, was a key figure in driving Iacocca's vision. Since that time, Chrysler has experienced continuing success culminating in being named "Company of the Year" in 1998 by *Forbes* magazine. Iacocca's vision was achieved in the latter part of 1998 when Chrysler merged with Daimler-Benz of Germany to become DaimlerChrysler. The continuing success of Chrysler is based on the visionary leadership established by Lee Iacocca and continued by the present Co-Chairman of DaimlerChrysler, Robert Eaton.

Transformative leadership is the ability to create a learning organization. Employees are naturally driven to embrace personal transformation as a requirement for continuous learning. They realize that accessing new knowledge is dependent on their detachment from current thinking. The key skills are problem solving, critical thinking, and creativity.

The Donnelly Corporation is an international automotive supplier serving every major automotive manufacturer around the world. The company is located in Holland, Michigan, and has 5,500 employees. They supply automotive components such as mirrors, windows, door handles, and interior trim and lighting. Donnelly established participative management in the early 1950s. The company is organized around ten business systems such as production, quality, program management, etc. The business systems are linked together through a program called Management by Planning (MBP), in which 100% of the employees participate. The MBP program is a five-phase process:

1. Vision

2. Long-term strategy

3. Fiscal-year objectives

4. Target actions

5. Supportive review

Integrated into the five-phase process is a series of tool boxes for implementation:

1.   Quality Tools

2.   Creativity Tools

3.   Decision-making Tools

For example, one of the business objectives might be to achieve a given market share of electrochromic mirrors. This objective sets in motion the input from other business units, such as total cost estimates, how to achieve sales objectives, or how to reduce launch time from 90 to 60 days. Critical thinking is involved in determining what is the reality of achieving the established market share. The Quality Tools skills involve critical thinking. The Creativity Tools are used for exploring the possibilities and thought processes in generating options for decisions. Many of the Creativity Tools involve the skill techniques of Dr. Edward DeBono.

The objective of the Donnelly operation is to fully utilize the talents and creativity of its diverse work force. The results of their operation in recent years are interior mirrors integrated with electronic features such as map lights, compasses, and electrochromic technologies that dim mirrors automatically to reduce glare. One of Donnelly's latest innovations, the IlluminatorTM outside mirror, incorporates a ground illuminator light, a supplemental turn signal, and an automatic dimming mirror into a single unit. These examples are major features of a learning organization that considers problem solving, critical thinking, and creativity to be the heart of its operation.

Spiritual leadership is the ability to inspire others to behave consistent with their highest moral and ethical values in the way they live and work with others.

These values include empathy, compassion, humility, and love. Although there are sound business reasons for operating in the manner discussed throughout this book, spiritual leaders do not need a business justification. They are driven by an *innate* sense of doing what is right, irrespective of the consequences. It is a moral violation of their ethics as a human being to live in opposition to their spiritual values.

Synovus Financial Corp. is an example of an organization that practices spiritual leadership. The company is based in Columbus, Georgia, and is comprised of 9,500 employees referred to as team members. The chairman of the executive committee, Bill Turner, openly speaks of love in the way the organization does its day-to-day business. He is described as the moral compass of the organization. Chairman and CEO Jim Blanchard espouses that within a team member's life their "God" or "Maker" comes first, their family second, and their job is third. Sonny Deriso, vice chairman states, "Everyone in a leadership position needs to live the values that we stand for, such as, doing the right thing, following the golden rule, having respect for others, and establishing an environment of trust."

Synovus' four leadership expectations include:

1) Live the values.

2) Share the vision.

3) Make others successful.

4) Manage the business.

Sonny states that spirituality has a lot to do with the incorporation of these four leadership expectations. He and Jim Blanchard talk regularly with team leaders about spiritual practices, such as those discussed above. He believes that if the organization operates in this way they will also do an exceptional job of serving their customers. Sonny believes that this way of operating has led to Synovus' economic and financial success. Their earnings for 1998 were $187 million, an increase of 13.4% as compared to 1997. Synovus was #1 on the 1999 Fortune Magazine list of *The 100 Best Companies to Work for in America*. They were also among the top 20 of Forbes' Platinum Businesses in Banking in the U.S. for 1999.

The new requirement for the New Leadership is spirituality. Spirituality goes beyond an intellectual recollection of historical values written by those who have had such a transformation. It even goes beyond belief in these historical values, no matter how altruistic the values or their written source may be. *Spiritual leadership is a way of being and is sourced from wisdom through spiritual transformation.*

Spiritual leadership requires a new kind of courage that has not traditionally been required of executives, managers, and employees. It requires the courage to look within for those values that serve everyone—employees, customers, and shareholders—and the willingness to take action to *ensure* that these values are practiced as everyday business functioning. The following section presents a spiritually sourced value system that drives high performance.

High Performance Is a Spiritual Pursuit

The model we proposed for creating a high-performance organization (page 22) is a spiritual pursuit when each of the initiatives is defined and practiced from a spiritual perspective. Each of these definitions is assumed to be *inherent* in every human being, whether practiced or not. Therefore, the definitions below should be read by inserting the word "inherent" after "the" in each of the statements below.

- *Teamwork* acknowledges the relatedness of people.

- *Quality* acknowledges the drive to achieve perfection.

- *Work Process Redesign* acknowledges the drive to continually improve systems, processes, and ourselves.

- *Environmentalism* acknowledges the connectedness of humans, animals, and the environment.

- *Customer Focus* acknowledges the desire to serve others.

- *Diversity* acknowledges the value of *all* people.

- *Empowerment* acknowledges the unlimited potential of the human spirit.

These statements are an example of a spiritually sourced value system for leadership and management. The difference between leadership and management is that leadership is principally a *way of being* and management is a *way of doing*. Therefore, leadership is spiritually oriented and management is principle and behavior oriented. The two are inseparable dimensions of leadership in action. There will always be a need for both to successfully operate an organization. The flow is *from* spirit *to* principle *to* behavior *to* results as shown below.

Spirit ⟶ Principle ⟶ Behavior ⟶ Results

The results in terms of profit, productivity, and support of people (measurables of a high-performance organization) are feedback to determine whether an organization's operation is either survival-driven or spiritually-driven. Therefore, high performance is the result of integrating humanistic principles and behaviors with sound business functioning, driven by a spiritual value system.

Spiritually Driven Principles and Behaviors of High Performance

The following list is an example of a corresponding set of principles and behaviors that follow from the spiritually sourced value system discussed in the previous section.

Teamwork is valued and rewarded in all aspects of our operation. It involves learning the values and workstyles of other team members and integrating them with your own to create high performance.

Quality is measured by how we continually exceed customers' expectations in every product or service we deliver. It includes measuring every product or service we produce in an effort to achieve zero-defect efficiency.

Work Process Redesign is a programmed component of all of our work and service processes. It includes brainstorming, upgrading any mature work process, and introducing information technology where possible.

Environmentalism is caring for the environment in such a way that its health sustains the well-being of *all* of Earth's inhabitants. This means continually monitoring ways of conserving energy and waste, and managing the impact of all processes on people and the environment.

Customer focus is making customers the center of everything we do. Utilizing customer feedback to upgrade job descriptions as well as continually improving service are essential ways of implementing this principle.

Diversity is valuing differences and integrating them into our core business functions. It includes the conscious avoidance of discriminatory behavior and seeking out the experience of differences in people, thinking, and workstyles.

Empowerment is leveraging the total capacity of our people in creating a high-performance organization. This includes delegating stretch projects in proportion to competency, while providing a committed leadership support system.

Leadership and a Global Perspective

As worldwide corporations progress through the stages of:

International—characterized by a centralized operation; to

Multinational—characterized by worldwide independently operating business units; to

Global—characterized by transnational integration and alignment of strategy, structure, culture, and people;

it is clear that harnessing the cooperation and synergism of radically different cultures will be *the* greatest challenge. Core cultures, in most of the world, have their genesis in centuries of tradition. They tend to be less flexible than younger cultures such as the United States.

The major problem affecting globalization is ethnocentrism—the human tendency to believe that one's culture and way of life is superior to others. Fortunately, this way of thinking is not dominant in most global business transactions. There has been clear intention to understand, value, and learn the worldview of others. This openness has set the stage for the new global paradigm of business which will be a *synthesis* of the Western and non-Western worldviews shown on the next page.

High context or low context refers to how information or knowledge is communicated in human transactions or relationships. A high context culture is one in which there is little or no information in the verbal or written messages. Most of the meaning is assumed to exist by the nature of the situation. Examples of high context cultures are those of South America, Asia, Africa, and the Middle East.

A low context culture is one where most of the information is in the verbal or written message to make up for what is missing in a situation. Low context cultures require extensive detailed explanations and information. Examples of low context cultures are those of England, Northern Europe, and North America (excluding Mexico).

Low Context/High Context Global Values

U.S. American Core Values (Low Context)	Non-Western Core Values (High Context)
• Individualism	• Group
• Equality	• Individual Dignity
• Democracy	• Consensus
• Personal Freedom	• Obligation to Others
• Fairness	• Fate (Karma, Joss)
• Achievement	• Process/Role
• Innovation	• Continuous Improvement
• Entrepreneurship	• Communal
• Competition	• Cooperation

The scale on the following page illustrates the context continuum as defined by Edward T. Hall.[9]

Low Context/High Context Continuum

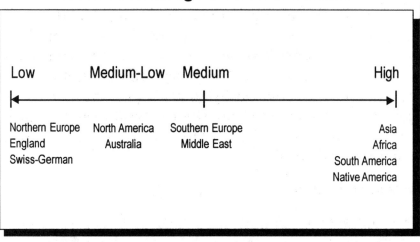

The following paragraphs describe the U.S. American core values and how they relate to business operation as shown on the previous page.

Individualism

Individualism is the perception of oneself as the cultural quantum of society. Therefore, self-interest, self-perception, self-motivation, and the freedom of self-expression have traditionally prioritized U.S. Americans' participation in the workplace.

Equality

Equality is the basic assumption that each individual is inherently of value because of her or his fundamental existence. Therefore, U.S. Americans tend to be informal, use first names irrespective of rank, assume there are no limitations to achievement, and take for granted that equal opportunity *ought* to be available to everyone.

Democracy

Democracy is based upon the assumption that the individuals who comprise the group should determine how they are governed. The government exists to assure individual freedoms, rights, security, and protection, but should not interfere unduly in their personal lives. In spite of these societal assumptions, until recently, most U.S. corporations have operated according to the hierarchical/military model.

Personal Freedom

Personal freedom is the assumption of unlimited self-expression and the rejection of overt authority over people, processes, and things. Individualism and equality are expressed in terms of achievements. Value of self is often equated to achievements. Thus, most U.S. Americans are achievement and goal-driven.

Fairness

U.S. Americans believe in due process and the opportunity for the individual to have rights respected, particularly when one is in the "underdog" position. The moral arguments for diversity—the assumption of equal opportunity and equality on teams—are examples of how this value plays out in the workplace.

Achievement

Achievement is the dominant motivation of U.S. American fulfillment and is often equated to the value of oneself. Therefore, U.S. Americans tend to be "doing oriented," focused on "getting something accomplished," and constantly seeking new, challenging projects more difficult than the last.

Innovation

Innovation is the natural result of constantly identifying or establishing more challenging goals and identifying process solutions with the value of the person. Thus, U.S. Americans tend to be ingenious in devising technical solutions, sophisticated devices and process improvement measurements (e.g., Six Sigma), and new management systems (e.g., performance-based management).

Entrepreneurship

Entrepreneurship is the natural result of the strong U.S. core values involving risk-taking, innovation, and individual fulfillment. Thus, the U.S. is still the world's center for new business ventures and intrapreneurship efforts within organizations.

Competition

Competition is the primary motivation of most U.S. Americans. It is driven by individualism, entrepreneurship, and achievement. Thus, among and within organizations, competition is often used as the primary motivator for achieving success.

Non-Western Core Values and Business Operation

The following paragraphs describe non-Western core values on page 193 and how they relate to business operation.

Group

Group is the perception that the group (e.g., family, company, or club) is the basic unit of society and that the individual is given meaning through identification with the group. Therefore, *keiretsus* are the obvious way to do business in Japan, and family association (nepotism) in business is most important in South America and Mexico. Keiretsus are cooperative business arrangements, even among competitors in Japan. In both situations, loyalty to the company is one of the greatest values and provides a sense of belonging to the group. Germany, as well as Japan, views business as an alliance among finance, business, and government. The focus is on the welfare of the society.

Individual Dignity

Individual dignity is the basic assumption that individuals are born into a position within the scheme of things, should make the most of their lot, and simply accept their position as the way it is. Thus, authoritarian business roles are extremely important in both Japan and China. Class systems are still active in India, as well as in Britain and Western Europe. Business roles and titles are formal and play a vital role in one's rise up the business hierarchy.

Consensus

Consensus is a collective position of a group arrived at by a process of dialogue which integrates all points of view. Therefore, Japanese business decision making appears to be painfully long by American standards. Self-directed teams, with the assumption of team member equality, often force high-involvement consensus decision making.

Obligation to Others

Obligation to others assumes that one is never totally free to act in one's self-interest if an individual is "one with the group." Obligation to the group is more important than one's own self-interest. Non-Western teams discourage individualism, espouse uniformity and conformity in behavior and dress, and focus on a smoothly functioning collective unit. In business, long-term give-and-take relationships are established, most small businesses are family units, and one's career and life are often guided by one's obligation to family.

Fate

Fate, from a Western perspective, is a view of life in which "life happens to people." Viewed from a non-Western perspective, there are "forces" that transcend an individual's ability to control which result in events that are beyond cause and effect, i.e., *the fates, joss,* or *karma.* There is no fairness or unfairness involved, it is simply one's fate. Even illness, fatigue, or family situations which may affect job performance are viewed as beyond the control of the individual. Therefore, the focus is on adapting to and accepting situations rather than attempting to change them.

Process/Role

Process/role is the quality of an individual's participation within the group without the necessity of personal reward. The focus is on the appropriateness and quality of relationship *during* the process rather than the achievement of a goal in the future. Therefore, such an individual would be motivated in a totally different way than a typical U.S. American. Value is placed on social relationships, group, and the *process* of achieving a goal.

Continuous Improvement

Continuous improvement is the natural result of continually improving one's self which results in both a better product and a better person; hence, the South Korean *kanban*, catchball management, and the Japanese Kaizen focus on quality as synonymous with worker improvement and performance rather than primarily the process or the system.

Communal

Communal small business ventures are spawned within the framework of a *keiretsu*, rather than an individual pursuing an idea. Entrepreneurship exists only within the framework of a web of larger business relationships; hence, the small Chinese family businesses in the U.S. and Canada having ties to mainland China, Hong Kong, and Taiwan.

The following pages list a set of practical leadership principles and behaviors that are consistent with the spiritual principles discussed in this chapter.

Leadership Principles and Behaviors

The following is a list of principles and behaviors for implementing the New Leadership consistent with the spiritual values described in this chapter.

1. Establish a personal vision of your function in concert with the organization's vision—use meditation and visualization to explore your creative consciousness for a vision that is consistent with your higher purpose, beyond self-interest.

2. Plan your work in concert with the vision of the organization—create specific, definable, and measurable results that would ensure that your personal vision is achieved.

3. Obstacles or difficulties, no matter how great, are opportunities in disguise to "catapult" your spiritual growth—use introspection for solutions or seek the assistance of a mentor who is versed in spiritual growth.

4. Support those you manage by learning of their aspirations—connect their expectations of success to the business objectives of the organization as part of their performance review.

5. At all times, put the organization's survival and success before your own personal interests—take responsibility to *always* be aware of the organization's financial health and volunteer ways to help through self-sacrifice.

6. Emotionally focus and intentionally create the reality of what you desire—write in detail what you

desire, read it every day, and do at least *one* activity in alignment with what you have written. If you don't do these things, your intention is really a desire, and has no power of manifestation.

7. Generously share profits with employees and the community within which you reside—design a profit-sharing plan that preserves the health of the business, employees, and the community.

8. Where necessary to manage others, manage with empathy, compassion, humility, and love (see page 91)—be humanistic in the way you facilitate employee development and performance.

9. Value and integrate differences in all your business transactions—establish an accountability system that is performance results-oriented in terms of differences.

10. Establish regular communication with your personal source of guidance, wisdom, and inspiration—take 5 to 15 minutes every day to meditate, pray, or introspect regarding a situation or opportunity that requires attention in your life.

Chapter Eight

The Future—A Call for Action

*"At a time when the world seems to be
spinning hopeless and out of control—
there are deceivers, and believers,
and old in-betweeners that seem to have
no place to go."*

Willie Nelson

Introduction

We have some tough decisions to make and we don't have much time. I would arbitrarily guess that we have about 10-20 years remaining before the environmental and cultural crises that we have set in motion over the past 100 years become irreversible. From an environmental standpoint, we need to stop pretending that we are not on a collision course with making the planet uninhabitable for human existence. Plants and animal species have become extinct, forests have been reduced to a fraction of what previously existed, and few rivers are free of dams and pollution. With unrestrained development and growth, grazing land, farmland, and wetlands are disappearing at an alarming rate. Much of the rapid expanse of commercialization has led to irreversible air and water pollution.

From a cultural standpoint, the impact of colonialism over the past centuries has also had a devastating effect on native, indigenous cultures, as well as the habitats in which they have traditionally lived. The major impact has been systematic extermination, particularly in the North, Central, and South Americas. The same is probably true in other parts of the world. In addition, we have still not learned, as a world society, to transcend ethnocentrism, racism, and sexism. We have had 10,000 wars in the last 5,000 years; almost totally as a result of our ethnocentric beliefs. And today, wars rage and will continue to rage until we dramatically transform as a human species. As a whole, we are still predominately driven by selfishness, greed, and competition. These characteristics, combined with the "isms" above, have led to a world of haves and have-nots; where the haves possess as high as 80% of the resources of the planet, even though they comprise less than 20% of the total population. In this final chapter, we will discuss the following subjects: our responsibility for the global consciousness; the challenge of "inner space" exploration; fundamental questions we must ask about our present belief structures; and what we can do, individually and collectively, to transform the consciousness of the planet into one that compatibly works for the future existence of humankind.

Taking Responsibility for the Consciousness of the Planet

The essence of the Spiritual paradigm is the realization that we require a major shift in our evolvement as a species. If we honestly examine the results of our existence over several thousand years, we have not made much progress in caring for the environment or for each other. Our own personal interests appear to be of greater importance in preference to the lot of others. Granted, there have been acts of compassion, legislation intended to alter behavior, and even the creation of world bodies to address our collective conflicts. *However, the context of planetary existence has not changed!* We have only improved the content, which is primarily in the area of technological development. Both a radical change in our behaviors as well as in our beliefs and values are necessary for a shift in human consciousness.

How do we begin this quest to have human consciousness catch up with technological advancement? By individually and collectively accepting 100% responsibility for the conditions that exist in our own lives as well as any aspect of humankind we can influence. For example, the shooting and killing of 15 high school students in Littleton, Colorado in April of 1999, should not be viewed as an isolated incident, separate and apart from each of us. We collectively, as a nation, support the consciousness of violence by the books we read, movies we attend, video games we play, television programs we view, toys we buy for our children, and the extent to which we ourselves are violent. And yet, with respect to Littleton, Colorado, we ask questions like, "How could this happen?" The fact is, we all know the answer to this question but few of us are willing to tell the truth. Probably, there is no universal answer for all of us but it is clear, by results, that the planetary consciousness is dominated by violence.

The point is, we are heading toward a self-destructive planetary scenario unless we collectively decide to significantly alter our present course. For example, whenever we experience injustice and violence in the world, ultimately, our most common response is "violent corrective action." This is an indication that the *system* is unworkable rather than the methods of response. The responses we may have, within our present context of thinking, are probably the best available. The bombing of the former republic of Yugoslavia by NATO forces which began in April, 1999, is a prime example of this point. Until we recognize and acknowledge our collective condition, we will remain in a coma.

Would You Help a Critically Ill Friend?

A friend confided to me recently, "The planet (or humankind) is like a critically ill patient in a coma." I agreed. In order to survive, we first have to come out of the coma. That can only be achieved by telling the truth. The truth is, we are a violent people. We have not evolved to the point of having mastery of our survival instincts. Only through the process of claiming responsibility for the condition of the planet will we be able to create solutions to ensure our continued existence. In fact, we will probably have to go through the Elizabeth Kübler-Ross process, described in Chapter Three, of *denial, reaction, bargaining, guilt,* and *acceptance.*

At this point, we have not decided whether we intend to save the patient or not. The most difficult part of this decision is having the *humility* to admit that we really don't know how to make things work within our present systems and belief structures. That perhaps, the latter are no longer valid for the way the world society functions today. *Our scientific, technical, and medical advancements have far out-distanced our present ability to manage these advancements responsibly.* Hence, the necessity for spiritual transformation. The greatest challenge we face today is not conquering "outer space," but mastering the "inner space" of human consciousness. For we humans on planet Earth, the next great frontier is a quantum jump in our collective evolvement to create a world that works for everyone.

Taking Action

Action begins with each of us examining our minute-to-minute and day-to-day living to discover how we each either contribute to the consciousness of a dysfunctional planet of people or systematically live consistent with harmony and love. The latter terms may sound "soft," however, they are the critical criteria by which we might measure our progress.

The relationship between the observable conditions of the planet and the planet's human consciousness is shown by the diagram below.

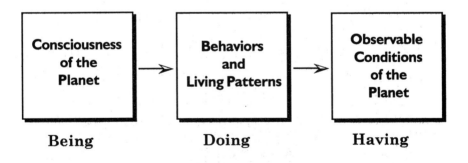

Consciousness of the Planet		Behaviors and Living Patterns		Observable Conditions of the Planet
Being		**Doing**		**Having**

What we observe as a result of our living pattern is a reflection of our collective thinking—both consciously and unconsciously. Our individual and collective consciousness drive our behaviors, both within ourselves and with others. Our behaviors, in turn, produce the results we observe. For example, a major concern in the U.S. is crime. In spite of the fact that we have the total resources to prevent widespread crime—that is, to feed, clothe, house, and provide everyone meaningful opportunities to lead successful lives—whatever it is we are *doing* is insufficient to significantly change this persistent condition. Our response to widespread crime, in our present paradigm of thinking, is to hire more enforcement officers, develop more sophisticated anti-crime technology, build more jails, and even implement well-meaning humanistic programs. It's obvious we need to begin asking serious and very difficult questions in terms of redesigning our fundamental belief structures for planetary existence, such as:

1) Does every human being have an *inherent right* to be fed, clothed, and sheltered whether he or she chooses to work or not?

2) Does the welfare of the group *supercede* the personal interests of the individual? No individual is free to acquire unlimited resources at the expense of the group—as reflected by the observable conditions of the planet.

3) Is it a flawed premise that business enterprise should always be *driven by growth*? Is there such a condition called enough? Particularly, since the planet and its resources are finite!

4) Is competition *inherently toxic* and ultimately *self-defeating*? And is cooperation a reflection

of an expanded level of consciousness that acknowledges our inherent connectedness? And possibly the ultimate key to our survival?

5) Is survival of the fittest a *human survival-based invention* designed to maintain the high imbalance of the haves and have-nots of the planet? And, in fact, the rest of the planet (animal, plant, and mineral kingdoms) operate in a *mutually compatible* "living and dying" cycle—which is not, at all, driven by survival.

6) And most fundamentally, do humans truly *have dominion* over other animals and the environment? Or, are we simply part of an overall web of intricate animate and inanimate relationships?

The ultimate question is:

7) Do we have the *courage* and the *humility* to transform our prevailing belief structures (consciousness of the planet) to compatibly exist on Earth?

This is perhaps the most difficult question for us, as humans, to proactively explore!

What Can We Do?

After serious and non-superficial examination of the questions in the previous section, we might begin by asking ourselves the following *personal* questions based upon our day-to-day behaviors. "No" answers affirm one's commitment to compatibly adapting to and preserving the planet for human habitancy.

- Do I waste food?

- Do I consume more resources than I need?

- Do I waste electricity, i.e., T.V., radio, lights, etc.?

- Do I gossip about others?

- Do I commonly experience conflict with people who have a different value system than mine?

- Do I incite reactionary behaviors from others, i.e., road rage, conflicts, etc.?

- Do I leave the water running when I brush my teeth?

- Do I waste materials and resources at work?

- Am I more concerned with personal gain than the welfare of others?

- Do I use the dishwasher (excessive water usage) unnecessarily?

- Do I spend excessive time and money on my appearance?

- Do I constantly behave in a way to prove that I am superior to others?

- Do I bear more children than the planet can nurture and support?

- Do I use profanity as a regular part of my vocabulary?

"Yes" answers to the following questions affirm one's commitment to compatibly adapting to and preserving the planet for human habitancy:

- Do I attempt to positively influence others?

- Do I spend time in the environment going on hikes or preserving nature?

- Do I obey traffic rules designed for public safety, i.e., speed limits?

- Do I create time for personal centering?

- Do I have a consciously planned focus for my life that preserves life and the environment?

- Do I pick up trash wherever I encounter it?

- Do I consume healthy foods and liquids?

- Do I exercise?

- Do I spend time influencing my siblings on win/win conflict resolution?

- Do I call attention to others about wasting resources and materials at work and home?

- Do I give back time, energy, and money to my community?

- Do I maintain sanitation at home and work?

- Am I *more* a citizen of the world than a citizen of my country?

- Am I tolerant and open to different cultures ideologically different from mine?

Given these sets of questions, you can create a set that is more personal and meaningful to your life. I encourage you to do so. Then, let them serve as a new guideline for your day-to-day living.

What Is the Responsibility of Our Global Business System?

Perhaps the greatest potential for transforming the consciousness of humankind is our global business system. Businesses, unlike any other societal system, have the resources (money), influence, and ability to act decisively, once a commitment is made. Business transcends borders, differing ideologies, and economic conditions like no other societal system. Probably because it is the societal system designed to provide us the personal resources we require for human survival. When *true* survival is at stake, we tend to change in the shortest period of time in whatever way necessary to sustain our existence.

Business organizations also respond quickly and decisively to change when their own survival is at stake. Driven by competitive survival and profitability, business organizations continue to push the limits of human adaptability. The indirect, but significant, result is accelerated human transformation in concert with the accelerated change in the business environment. These statements are perhaps best captured by Bill Gates' 1999 book titled *"Business @ The Speed of Thought."*

How can the global business system take the lead in addressing our challenge of transforming human consciousness? We might begin with the following suggestions:

1) Create spirituality within your organization— *be an example.*

2) Create forums for transforming the planetary consciousness—*raise awareness.*

3) Pay employees for community service on company time—*give back to the community.*

4) Seek to operate more in cooperation rather than pitted competition—*create a consciousness of cooperation.*

5) Create a speaker series on "Creating a Consciousness of Planetary Caring, Compatibility, and Cooperation"—*promote the transformation of human evolvement.*

6) Create meditation rooms in the workplace— *encourage employees to constructively download workplace frustrations and conflict.*

7) Create a new value system that includes humanistic principles—*integrate humanistic values with sound business functioning.*

8) Establish education and training on spirituality in the workplace—*provide transformative opportunities for the work force.*

9) Sponsor sabbaticals for employees to learn and employ spiritual workplace principles and practices—*develop leadership practices for employing spirituality in the workplace.*

10) Consciously work to create a context of planetary cooperation where *every human soul* is adequately fed, clothed, and sheltered on a

continual basis—*create a consciousness of a world that works for everyone.*

Creating Our Reality

Where change and adaptation to change are concerned, this is the point: "*We create our individual and collective realities right down to the significant and insignificant details.*" As Professor Leland Kaiser of the University of Colorado business school stated, "How quickly can you change your reality?" Answer: "As quickly as it takes to change your mind." Although I have focused on the business system as leading the charge for cultural transformation, government, parents, schools, special interest groups, and each of us have roles to play. The question we must continually ask is, "How must we restructure our society to preserve humanity *and* ensure quality of life for *everyone?*"

I don't have the answers to this question, but I *know* collectively we do. A basic rule of life is: "There is no problem created by humankind that cannot be solved by the individual and collective minds of human beings." The challenging question is, do we have the courage to bring forth the solutions and implement them? This is the greatest test of ourselves as we enter the 21st Century.

I choose to end this ongoing dialogue with the questions I have posed for each of us to address. I am confident that our continued evolvement as a human species will prevail!

The following page lists practical ways that you might use for creating a context (consciousness) of spirituality in the workplace.

Creating a Context of Spirituality in the Workplace

1. Commit yourself to an in-depth process of self-discovery to learn your spiritual values.

2. Create a list of actions and behaviors consistent with your spiritual values—and live them!

3. Integrate your values and ethics with important business decisions you make. Ask yourself, "Is this the right thing to do?"

4. Create a personal wellness program that includes eating, exercise, health, recreation, and a balanced life.

5. Trust others in a responsible way without the necessity of proof.

6. Dedicate yourself to a program of continuous learning by choosing stretch projects with coaching.

7. Commit to bring your whole self to work every day—body, mind, and spirit.

8. Use teaming as an opportunity for interpersonal growth.

9. Instead of automatically expecting more money, assess your value-added performance; and then decide if you merit more money.

10. Focus your thoughts and actions on the things you can change or influence—leave the rest to the Laws of Karma!

The Appendices include responses to "Questions People Ask about Spirituality in the Workplace" that I have collected over several years. They also include a self-test to determine how spiritual you are as well as a step-wise process for integrating spirituality into your organizational culture. Your comments are invaluable regarding anything discussed in this book. You might communicate them via:

William A. Guillory
Innovations International, Inc.
310 East 4500 South, Suite 420
Salt Lake City, Utah 84107

Appendix A
Questions People Ask about Spirituality and the Workplace

Q: What is spirituality?

A: Spirituality is that which comes from within, beyond the survival instincts of the mind. Each of us has a spiritual center, which is our connection to this source of inner knowing.

Q: What do you mean by a "spiritual center?"

A: A spiritual center is our inner core self—beyond our *programmed* beliefs and values—that is the source of wisdom. It is the source that influences us to behave with passion, understanding, empathy, humility, compassion, and love.

Q: What does the word "spiritual" mean?

A: That which is spiritual:

- comes from one's inner self.

- benefits self and others.

- creates alignment of purpose/people.

- comes with surety (validated by the heart).

- creates inner meaning and motivation about work.

- creates inner peace in one's self; centeredness.

- is a *natural* desire to help others grow, learn, and succeed.

- respects and values individual and group dignity.

Q: Is there a difference between spirituality and religion?

A: Yes. Spirituality is "essence" and religion is "form." Spirituality is the source of an unlimited number of forms the human experience may take, such as meditation, prayer, Zen, environmental conservation, and treating others with respect, dignity, and as equals.

Q: What is the relationship between spirituality and work life?

A: Work life has become so demanding, fast paced, stressful, ambiguous, and chaotic that we are forced to seek values-based answers and ways of achieving personal stability from within. We have come to realize that our inner wisdom is the *only* source that will sustain our adaptation and stability in the long run.

Q: How does spirituality show up in the workplace?

A: Workplace activities that are spiritually sourced include:

- Bereavement programs.

- Wellness information displayed and distributed.

- Employee Assistance Programs.

- Programs that integrate work/family.

- Management systems that encourage personal and spiritual transformation.

- Servant leadership—the desire to serve others first in preference to self.

- Stewardship—leadership practices that support the growth and well-being of others.

- Diversity programs that create inclusive cultures.

- Integration of core values and core business decisions and practices.

- Leadership practices that support the growth and development of *all* employees.

Q: What are workers experiencing that requires spirituality as a work force necessity?

A: The necessity for spirituality has intensified because of the pressures of today's workplace in terms of:

- Personal Stability—surviving/adapting to the chaotically changing workplace.

- Balancing Work/Personal Life—revisiting what's important to us and reprioritizing our life activities (based upon spirituality sourced values).

- Greater Performance—need for continuous learning driven from an inner passion.

- Work as Meaning—given today's workplace pressures, employees are asking, "What's meaningful work for me?"

- Work Force Reduction—an increasing need to do more in less time.

- Humanistic Organizational Cultures—the connect (or disconnect) between an individual's personal values and the organization's practiced values.

- Self-Management—the need to solve our own problems through greater empowerment and creativity.

Solutions to these challenges require "inner space" exploration and resolution. *Inner space exploration and resolution is a spiritual process! Inner space refers to one's spiritual center.*

Q: **What is the relationship between spirituality and the workplace?**

A: In order to compensate for the loss of job security and the continuing need for high-performing employees, today's productive and profitable workplaces require organizational cultures that integrate humanistic core values with core business policies, decisions, functions, and behaviors; cultures that support the physical, mental, and spiritual well-being of its employees.

Q: **What is the role of leadership in promoting spirituality?**

A: 1) Appoint a committee to define how spirituality plays out in your organization—including an appropriate definition of "spirituality in our workplace."

2) Define how spirituality is (or can be) integrated into your strategic plan.

3) Do a Spirituality Survey.

4) Make certain your performance surveys include an evaluation of how effectively your organizational core values are practiced.

5) Create an environment of trust—where employees feel safe to question, learn, and contribute.

6) Require personal development seminars—including values clarification and expected humanistic behaviors.

7) Be an example of the humanistic values you expect of others.

8) Promote diversity because it is a moral and ethical statement of your *spiritual* belief in human equality.

Q: How do you overcome the challenge of living/working in a workplace where spiritual principles are not valued or practiced?

A: First, realize that integrating spirituality into your life is for your personal benefit in terms of stress-reduction, centeredness, and personal stability. It is your source of personal adaptation in today's chaotically changing workplace and world.

Adapting to your present workplace practices begins with:

1) Redefining your five most important personal values that are spiritually sourced, such as family, personal time, creativity, religious practices, health, etc.

2) Defining your personal workplace values, such as money, equality, empowerment, respect, quality relationships, making a difference, etc.

3) Comparing your personal values with your perception of the practiced values of your workplace, such as competition, self-interest, control, hierarchy, as well as empowering humanistic values.

If your values and their values are significantly out of alignment, you have important decisions to make.

i) Remain and non-reactively accept your situation (because your workplace benefits are too great to give up).

ii) Remain and work to change the culture, accepting whatever consequences that may occur.

iii) Begin looking for a workplace that is more compatible with your values—then decide to leave or accept (i), or (ii).

iv) Start your own small business.

Ultimately, remember you are not required to participate in political games or other non-spiritual activities. Most of all, if you can identify with the pain others experience in counterproductive behaviors, your relationship and hence your influence with them will transform.

Q: How do individuals who accept and live spiritual values lead teams that have not moved into this realm?

A: i) Introduce the idea that humanistic team values are as important as business objectives in achieving team success.

ii) Don't use the word "spiritual" initially, if unnecessary. Use ethics, values, or morals.

iii) Do a brainstorming session where "spiritual" or "ethical values" are established as a working part of the team dynamics.

iv) Expose team members to "appropriate" spiritual literature that show the practical relationship between business success and spirituality, e.g., *Soul of the Firm* by C. William Pollard.

Q: Are the differences between spiritual goals and organizational goals compatible and possible to manifest? For example, a spiritual goal may be to fully develop employees, allowing and building upon the creativity of the individual. An organizational goal is usually to deliver a product on time and within budget. If an individual is not mastering the organizational goal fast enough, how does one stay connected to the spiritual goal?

A: First, spirituality is more about process—the way things are done—than it is about achieving goals. The development of an individual and building on creativity will naturally require spiritual practices *in the process* of achieving an organizational goal. The rate at which an individual grows is mostly self-determined. An organizational goal to deliver a product on time within budget may *force* or *inspire* an employee to learn new skills and assume greater responsibility in order to achieve that goal. In this sense, spiritual goals and organizational goals are not only compatible, but mutually beneficial.

Q: Because all organizations set specific (and frequently unrealistic) financial goals and objectives, how does an employee not move into "fear" concerning one's own survival?

A: Remember, fear is always sourced from a belief we have about ourselves that is usually unfounded. By exploring the worst case scenario regarding our fear and how we would adapt, the energy surrounding our fear is tremendously reduced. Survival really involves food, shelter, and clothing, and these are usually covered in most worst case scenarios. What we usually fear is a lack of income to sustain a certain "standard of living."

In the final analysis, our survival is dependent upon our ability to continually develop leading-edge skills that ensure employment.

Q: Fear-based management is often the driver in most companies. Such quotes as "do it right the first time" have been greatly misquoted in purpose and meaning. Now many employees fear making a mistake. Spirituality is the absence of fear. How does one move from the fear-driven culture to one of peace and love?

A: True, being centered in one's spiritual self is the absence of fear. Therefore, when fear is present we have uncoupled from our spiritual source and the survival instincts of the mind have taken over. If we are secure within ourselves of our inherent value of being human *and* our ability to contribute to the success of our organization, then fear-based management has no power. Again, exploring beliefs we may have around "perceived security" and *realizing* they are involved is how we become immune to fear-based management. The key realization is that peace and love are inner sourced, whether they are an inherent part of a culture or not.

Q: Spirituality is listening to our inner guidance and should be the greatest source for making decisions. How does one explain a decision made without the (illusory) facts to support the decision to management?

A: Many, or even most, important business decisions are not necessarily sourced from our inner guidance. Many are sourced from sound business reasoning or rationale. Operating effectively in today's workplace requires an ability to be "in the world" (because that's where we are) and "not of the world" (so that we can remain detached where appropriate).

In other words, depending on the person, it is rather easy to "create" rational, acceptable explanations for an intuitively sourced decision. For example, if an individual has a strong moral belief that "diversity is the right thing to do," then creating a strong business rationale on the basis of the effective utilization of the total work force is not that difficult. Although, it is clearly understood by that individual that their decision to become diverse is spiritually sourced. Connecting intuition with sound business rationale requires a good understanding of the business within which one is employed.

Q: How does an employee deal in a spiritual manner with his/her manager that has their own personal and egotistical agenda?

A: Where a manager's agenda does not adversely affect our ability or freedom to do our work effectively and efficiently, there is nothing *necessary* to do. We might first observe our own motivation for intolerance. *If* our own motivation comes from a righteous position, then our upset about that individual is a mirror reflection of characteristics we hide about ourselves.

When action and change is required, we begin by resolving "our own agenda" of why others should change. When an egotistical motivation is resolved, a *process* of engagement through conversations can be very effective. Ask questions of that person about their professional or business aspirations. What does he/she enjoy most about their job? What things do they find most difficult? (This question reveals their fears.) How could you be more *genuinely* supportive of helping with the business requirements? etc.

The essence in dealing with someone who has an egotistical agenda is captured in the definition of wisdom. *"Wisdom is an in-depth understanding, empathy, and compassion for the human experience."* From here, the appropriate action is usually obvious.

Q: **When an employee's company does not openly promote spirituality, how does one choose an appropriate mentor?**

A: Likes attract! (As do opposites in physics!)

1) Look for behavioral characteristics such as empathy, compassion, and humility.

2) Look for an individual described as a "people person," or one who has heart.

3) Make a list of three of these individuals who also have the ability and influence to promote your professional career. They should have both humanistic and professional credentials.

4) Schedule informal meetings with each of them and ask questions about *their* adaptation and future success.

5) *Listen with your heart!* Trust your intuition. At some point, step across the line and ask about their views on spirituality in the workplace. Sit back and listen. At this point your heart will guide you.

Q: How does an employee stay out of fear and stay centered when his/her entire career future is influenced by situations outside of his/her control, such as financial results, canceled projects, client business changes, acquisitions, etc.?

A: First of all, your future and your career are totally in *your* control. "You create your own reality." The theme of this question appears to be "fear of change." My experience is that when one of the changes cited above occurs, fear is inevitable. How we respond is key. Fear usually persists when we behave in ways of denial; such as being angry (denying responsibility), discussing the unfairness of the situation (feeling victimized), and a desperate hope that the change situation will not become reality. The objective is to move rapidly *through* this process to acceptance.

Being centered is the same as accepting reality. Now consider the worst case scenario. What would you do if it occurred? Would you survive? Would you have food, shelter, and clothing? Could you provide for yourself and your family? The more responsibility you take for your life, the less "things *happen* to you!"

Q: How does an employee, who is working as a team towards a common goal but is evaluated as an individual compared to his/her team members, resolve this conflict?

A: 1) Accept the fact that American corporations rarely, if ever, reward teamwork. Then work to change this practice.

2) Do a brainstorming session to show the cost benefits of teamwork as compared to 100% individual efforts, e.g., simultaneous engineering, cycle time reduction, customer service, and creativity and synergism.

3) Encourage your team to make a unanimous recommendation that your team project be X% for team success and Y% for individual contribution in terms of rewards or compensation.

4) Ultimately, recognize that the *conflict* is within you. It is the gap between how you believe it "should be" as compared to the reality of "how it is." When this inner conflict is resolved, what you should do becomes obvious.

Q: Because we were all raised in an academic world where individual grades were critical to our success, how does an employee shift from the mind-set of competition for advancement to the "spiritual mindedness" of what is good for all?

A: When competition is a motivation for self-improvement or greater performance, it can benefit everyone. Particularly where one has to call upon personal inspiration and creativity—both are spiritually sourced.

When competition is at the expense of others, it usually leads to win/lose or more often lose/lose. The present business mergers are a realization of the good for all in most cases. It reduces "pitted competition," which is inherently toxic. Within your organization:

1) Reduce the idea of fixed territorial jobs.

2) Disseminate all relevant business information freely.

3) Have frequent team/small department meetings and share responsibilities across personnel.

4) Publicize how everyone's effort was necessary for the success of a project.

Q: **What does an employee do when an error has been made and management chooses to cover it up from the customer?**

A: If the error involves you and you have direct communication with the customer, request your manager's permission to be honest with the customer. If your manager refuses, then write a memo of your request and your manager's response that is sent to him/her and you also retain a copy.

If the customer ultimately asks you about the error, tell the truth and be willing to accept whatever consequences there might be.

If your spiritual principles are important to your mental well-being, then at some point you will have to take a stand.

Q: **When honesty is a core value to an employee, how does this employee deal with an organization or management team where it is not?**

A: Raise the issue with the organization or team when violated. Determine if either plans to practice honesty in their business dealings. If continued violations occur, begin to consider your options.

Q: What do you do when you feel your ethics are being compromised?

A: First, be a visible example of your own spiritual values, e.g., don't participate in gossip, work efficiently, be empathic and compassionate to others, don't participate in politics, and take responsibility for your successes and non-successes.

Secondly, extend these practices in your interactions with others without being a self-appointed "Captain of the World."

In the final analysis, you must decide if you can "live with" the non-alignment of your ethics and your organization's ethics. If not, again, consider your options.

Q: Many corporate leaders are hesitant to speak of spirituality at all within the workplace due to its religious implications and that legal ramifications may result. How can this issue be addressed?

A: Appoint an organization-wide committee to explore how spirituality might impact your workplace, customers, or productivity. Include in this assignment a charge to define spirituality as it relates to your workplace—the same as you did with diversity.

Include your legal expert as part of the committee to ensure, as best you can, that legal problems are avoided. Then, have the CEO use this report as a basis for the discussion of spirituality and its workplace implications.

Q: Is it really possible for one person to make a difference or does it take an organizational commitment at a corporate level to have spirituality play a role in a company?

A: *Making a difference* is *not* measured by the magnitude of the event! Every act of transformation makes a difference—regardless of whether everyone else knows about it.

To transform a culture usually requires the efforts of many.

Q: What do you do if only one form of spirituality is valued at your workplace, e.g., European-based Christianity; Good Friday and Easter?

A: This is both a spiritual issue as well as a diversity issue. The best way to create valuation of other religious days is through a diversity initiative.

A diplomatic letter to your boss, vice president, or president might be a good way to get the process started. Ultimately, the discussion of holidays for all employees should be granted within an organization's policy.

For example, a Salt Lake City-based organization switched from Presidents Day to Martin Luther King Day as their official holiday for all employees.

How spiritual are you? Take the following quiz to find out.

1. In my opinion spirituality and religion are □ Yes □ No different.

2. I am passionate about my work most of □ Yes □ No the time.

3. I am actively open to personal growth □ Yes □ No when I encounter conflict.

4. I am active in contributing to the well- □ Yes □ No being of others in addition to myself.

5. I function, most of the time, consistent □ Yes □ No with my personal values in my workplace.

6. I use spiritual practices as a means of adapt- □ Yes □ No ing to my workplace stresses and demands.

7. I am 100% responsible for whatever hap- □ Yes □ No pens in my life, even if a situation is unfair.

8. I use my creativity and intuition on a regu- □ Yes □ No lar basis in both my personal and profes- sional life.

9. I ensure that my physical well-being is □ Yes □ No maintained by the foods I eat, regular physical activity, and preventative health measures.

10. Life, for me, is a "daring adventure" of □ Yes □ No personal and professional growth.

Instructions: Give yourself 10 points for each "Yes" response.

Score: 80 – 100 points

You are a very spiritual person who has a healthy attitude toward life. You are adaptable and continually learn from your experiences in personal and professional situations.

Score: 60 – 79 points

You are a spiritual individual who tends to limit your spirituality in confronting situations. You might gain greater confidence and value in your life by trusting more in your intuition from which wisdom is sourced.

Score: 40 – 59 points

You may be blocking your spirituality by attaching too much importance to material objectives. You may discover a wealth of satisfaction and well-being by getting to know your inner self better.

Score: Below 40 points

You probably find life to be a struggle for survival. You may have to make some difficult decisions in order to open your self to true happiness. The first step may be to take responsibility for the situation you are in and realize that only *you* can make it better.

Q: **How do I put spirituality into practice?**

A: 1) Take 5-10 minutes each day for "centering" yourself using some form of meditation or stress-reducing discipline.

2) When you experience a conflict with someone, take a deep breath, reflect, and validate your inherent value

as a human being as separate from the conflict you are experiencing.

3) Become consciously aware of how often you behave in conflict with your personal values that are spiritually sourced—then begin consciously behaving in ways that create alignment with your values.

4) Take creativity courses and apply your learning to day-to-day work life.

5) Whenever you make a business decision, compare it with your organization's core values. If in conflict, create processes that align with your organization's core values.

6) Be more compassionate of the shortcomings of others.

7) Be open to and seek out non-traditional methods of healing and wellness.

8) Become consciously aware of how you waste your organization's resources—pencils, paper, copies, phone time, work time, etc.—and adopt conservation behaviors.

9) Commit to appropriate forms of personal development —workshops, audiotapes, Yoga, Zen, prayer, support groups, etc.

10) Define (or create) ways to contribute to your community with no expected recognition, reward, or profit.

Appendix B
Integrating Spirituality into Your Organizational Culture

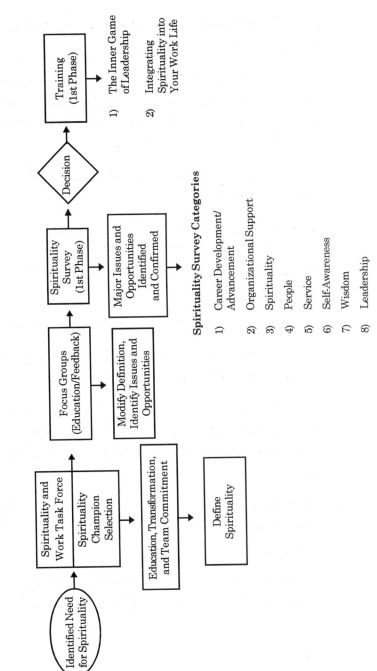

Spirituality Survey Categories

1) Career Development/ Advancement
2) Organizational Support
3) Spirituality
4) People
5) Service
6) Self-Awareness
7) Wisdom
8) Leadership

Appendix B
Integrating Spirituality into Your Organizational Culture—Continued

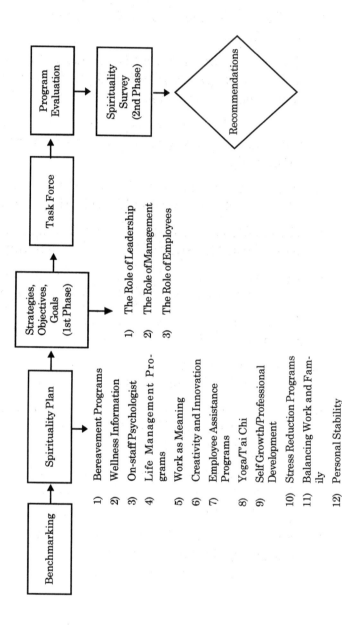

Benchmarking → Spirituality Plan → Strategies, Objectives, Goals (1st Phase) → Task Force → Program Evaluation → Spirituality Survey (2nd Phase) → Recommendations

1) The Role of Leadership
2) The Role of Management
3) The Role of Employees

1) Bereavement Programs
2) Wellness Information
3) On-staff Psychologist
4) Life Management Programs
5) Work as Meaning
6) Creativity and Innovation
7) Employee Assistance Programs
8) Yoga/Tai Chi
9) Self Growth/Professional Development
10) Stress Reduction Programs
11) Balancing Work and Family
12) Personal Stability

Bibliography

1. Guillory, William A., *The Guides*. Boulder City: R. K. Books,1997.

2. Guillory, William A. and Linda Galindo, *EMPOWER-MENT for High-Performing Organizations*. Salt Lake City: Innovations Publishing, Inc., 1996.

3. Greenleaf, Robert K., *The Servant As Leader*. India-napolis: Robert K. Greenleaf Center For Servant Leadership.

4. Patagonia: *Yvon's Diatribes*, 9/16/96:42:4, http:www.patagonia.com\lite\enviro\yvons.html.

5. Kübler-Ross, Elisabeth, *On Death and Dying*. New York: MacMillan Publishing Company,1970.

6. Maslow, Abraham, *Toward A Psychology of Being*. New York: Van Nostrand Reinhold Company, 1968.

7. Dent, Harry S., *The Great Boom Ahead*. New York: Hyperion, 1993.

8. Koestenbaum, Peter, *The Heart of Business*. Dallas: Saybrook Publishing, 1991.

9. Hall, Edward T. and Mildred Reed Hall, *Under-standing Cultural Differences*. Yarmouth: Intercul-tural Press, Inc., 1990.

10. Stewart, Edward C. and Milton J. Bennett, *American Cultural Patterns*. Yarmouth: Intercultural Press, Inc., 1991.

11. Renesch, John E., Editor, *Leadership in a New Era: Visionary Approaches to the Biggest Crisis of Our Times*. San Francisco: New Leaders Press, 1994.

About the Author

Dr. William A. Guillory is the CEO and founder of Innovations Consulting International, Inc. He has presented more than 4,000 seminars throughout corporate America, Europe, Mexico, and Canada. He has facilitated seminars for over 200 corporations, including the senior management of American Airlines, Avon Products, Inc., Eastman Kodak Company, Electronic Data Systems, Lockheed Martin Corporation, Sandia National Laboratories, Rohm and Haas Company, Texas Instruments, Pacific Enterprises, DaimlerChrysler, and Kellogg Corporation.

Dr. Guillory is an authority on diversity, empowerment, leadership, creativity, and quantum-thinking. He is a widely requested and popular conference and keynote speaker on these subjects as well as spirituality in the workplace. He is the author of four books on personal transformation, *Realizations, It's All an Illusion, Destined to Succeed,* and *The Guides,* and is the co-author of the management book entitled EMPOWERMENT *For High Performing Organizations.* He is also a member of the National Training Laboratory.

Prior to founding Innovations, Dr. Guillory was a physical chemist of international renown. He received his B.S. degree from Dillard University and his Ph.D. from the University of California at Berkeley. Following his doctoral work, Dr. Guillory was a National Science Foundation postdoctoral fellow at the University of Paris—The Sorbonne. He has lived, studied, and lectured in England, France, Germany, Japan, Switzerland, Poland, and China. He is the author of over one hundred publications and several books on the application of lasers in chemistry. He also served as Chairman of the Department of Chemistry at the University of Utah.

His distinguished awards and appointments include an Alfred P. Sloan Fellowship, an Alexander von Humboldt appointment at the University of Frankfurt, a Ralph Metcalf Chair at Marquette University, and the Chancellor's Distinguished Lectureship at the University of California at Berkeley. Dr. Guillory founded Innovations in 1985 following a period of intense personal growth which led to a career change to individual and organizational transformation.

Other Titles by William A. Guillory

Realizations

The Business of Diversity

The Global Manager

It's All an Illusion

EMPOWERMENT
*for High-Performing
Organizations*

Destined to Succeed

The Guides

Rodney — The Children's Series

*Rodney Goes to the Country —
The Children's Series*

Index

Index

Index

Q
Quality, 21, 189-191
Quantum-thinking, 97-100, 170-172

R
Re-creation, 80, 172
Relationship, 115, 117, 133
Relationship orientation, 124

S
Scandinavian Airlines System, 104
Self-awareness, 109, 115
Self-awareness instrument, 135-141
Self-management, 76, 114
Service, 83-84, 88, 114
Service performance evaluation, 106-108
Southwest Airlines, 99, 102
Sowell, Shaunna, 150-152
Spiritual Age, 97
Spirituality, 31-34, 56-57, 97
Spiritual communication, 117-118
Spiritual leadership, 77, 187-189

T
Task orientation, 124
Teamwork, 133
Texas Instruments, 150

TDIndustries, 23-24, 35-36
Toyota, 14-16
Transformation, 1, 41, 84, 113
Transformative leadership, 185-187
Trust, 124

U
UPS, 102-103

V
Vision, 172-173
Visionary leadership, 185

W
Wisdom, 59-60, 143-144, 148, 152

X
Xenophobia, 149

Innovations International, Inc.

Innovations is a global human resource development corporation specializing in personal and organizational transformation. We exist to provide the most advanced transformative technologies to corporations, globally, in order to assist them in prospering in the 21st Century.

Our specializations in consulting include:

- Diversity
- Empowerment
- Leadership
- Creativity and Innovation
- Quantum-thinking

These specializations include comprehensive programs involving consulting, seminars, audits and assessments, coaching, and interactive multimedia learning.

Our multimedia series in Diversity and High Performance feature CD-ROM interactive processes including video presentations and scenarios, question and answer discussions, interactive case studies, and self-management skills.

For information regarding Innovations' programs, telephone, write, fax, Email, or visit our web page:

Innovations International, Inc.
310 East 4500 South, Suite 420
Salt Lake City, UT 84107 USA
Tel (801) 268-3313
Fax (801) 268-3422
Email: Innointl@cris.com
Web Site: www.innovint.com